The Collaborative Construction of Pretend

SUNY Series,
Children's Play in Society

Anthony D. Pellegrini, Editor

The Collaborative Construction of Pretend

SOCIAL PRETEND PLAY FUNCTIONS

Carollee Howes
with
Olivia Unger and Catherine C. Matheson

STATE UNIVERSITY OF NEW YORK PRESS

Published by
State University of New York Press, Albany

© 1992   State University of New York

For information, address State University of New York
Press, State University Plaza, Albany, N.Y. 12246

Production by Ruth Fisher
Marketing by Theresa A. Swierzowski

Library of Congress Cataloging-in-Publication Data

Howes, Carollee.
  The collaborative construction of pretend : social pretend play
 functions / Carollee Howes, with Olivia Unger and Catherine C.
 Matheson.
   p. cm. — (SUNY series, children play in society)
  Includes bibliography (p.) and index.
  ISBN 0–7914–0755–1 (acid-free) . — ISBN 0–7914–0756–X (pb : acid
 -free)
  1. Play. 2. Imagination in children. I. Unger, Olivia.
 II. Matheson, Catherine C. III. Title. IV. Series.
 HQ782.H68 1992
 155.4' 18—dc20

                 90–10330
                    CIP

10 9 8 7 6 5 4 3 2 1

Contents

133012

PART III: Trust and Intimacy

1

Introduction

Imagine that you are visiting a child-care center. You begin in the yard where toddler-age children are playing in a sandbox. One child shapes a pile of sand into a "cake" and says "birthday" while a child beside her fills a cup with sand, raises it to his lips, and does not take a drink. In the three-year-olds' room a group of children are in the block corner near a long string of foot-long blocks. A girl says, "Pretend this is the magic snake." A boy says, "Yes, but it is a train snake and I am the engineer." In the four-year-olds' room you see children dressed in flowing gowns acting out a fantasy play with kings, queens, and princesses. One child informs you that he is the dragon, the princess is going to run away, and the king and the queen will hunt for her.

You may conclude from your visit that social pretend play is a favorite, if not an important activity of childhood. Psychologists, parents, and early childhood educators have long been interested in children's social pretend play. Research on children's play suggests that besides being fun and interesting for both the children and the adults who watch them, play has important educational implications. Children's social pretend play is linked to all aspects of development—emotional, cognitive, linguistic, and social. (See Johnson, Christie, & Yawkey 1987; and Rubin, Fein, & Vandenberg 1983 for reviews of this literature.) In this book we argue that the development of children's social competence, particularly of their competence in forming relationships with peers, is closely linked to their social pretend play.

The field of early peer relationships and friendships has been characterized by rich descriptive studies of relationship and interactive processes with little theoretical structure. Recently, Gottman and colleagues (Gottman & Mettetal 1986; Parker & Gottman 1989) and Howes (1987, 1988) proposed alternative models for the sequential development of social relationships with peers in childhood. These two models have much in common. Both models distinguish between friendships and social acceptance or popularity with peers. Both models propose that social competence with peers develops as children master particular social tasks or processes in their interaction with peers and that the social tasks change with development. These tasks or processes are called "marker behaviors" of social competence. Individual social competence may be assessed by the presence or absence of these developmental markers. Finally, both models suggest that social pretend play has a central role in the development of social relationships and social competence.

The two models appear to differ in their consideration of the role or function of social pretend play. Howes argues that social pretend play in the early toddler period (children between the ages of 24 and 36 months) represents the communication of meaning and thus is a marker of social competence in that period. She further suggests that the marker of social competence for children during the preschool period (three to five years of age) is social knowledge of the peer group. In her model, the central task for preschool children is to understand that they are part of a larger social group and to differentiate between friendship and playmate relationships within the group. In contrast, Gottman and colleagues argue that the central social task for three- to seven-year-old children is to achieve coordinated play, the highest level of which is fantasy or social pretend play. Within the Gottman model the social task of middle childhood (elementary school-age children) is a form of peer group integration, specifically, inclusion in the same-sex peer group. For elementary school children, gossip replaces social pretend play as the social task. Thus, Gottman and colleagues identify a longer period, ages three to seven, in which social pretend play is a salient social process. Furthermore, Howes uses social pretend play as a marker of social competence in the developmental period prior to the period identified by Gottman.

One way of resolving the discrepancies between the two models is to examine the following question: How can social pretend play be a marker of social competence with peers during the toddler period and still be elaborated during the three- to seven-year-old period? One easy answer to this question is definitional. Howes's definition of social pretend play is based on observation (Howes 1988; Howes, Unger, & Seidner 1989). In the most complex form of social pretend play used by Howes, children need only to use pretend actions to engage in complementary roles. Toddlers can communicate meaning in social pretend play without any use of language. Gottman's (1983) primary data source is audio transcripts. Thus, he relies on verbal transformations and script content to identify social pretend play. Therefore, Howes and Gottman examine different forms of social pretend play. These different forms are rooted in different developmental periods.

A more complex answer to the question of discrepancies between the Gottman and Howes models lies within the function or functions of social pretend play. Gottman ascribes an integrative function to social pretend play. Children use pretend play to establish and maintain social relationships. In contrast, Howes ascribes a communicative function to social pretend play. Pretend enriches social play through the communication of meaning.

In this book we will argue that social pretend play can fulfill several different developmental functions and that these functions change with development. If the function of social pretend play changes with development then social pretend play can be considered an important social task over a relatively long period in development. The Howes and Gottman models are not incompatible if the function of social pretend play changes with development. Within a developmental framework mastery of communication of meaning within social pretend play is the task of toddlers while the integration of social pretend play is the task of older children. We will argue that social pretend play is salient in the formation of both social interaction skills and friendships from the toddler period into middle childhood, but that there are changes in both the forms and the functions of social pretend play across these periods.

Fundamental Assumptions

Two fundamental assumptions underlie this argument. We have assumed that the development of social competence with peers can be described as a series of sequential social tasks or marker behaviors. The idea that the social tasks serve as markers of competent behavior and that these tasks or markers change across developmental periods is central to developmental psychology (Wolhwil 1973). By using marker behaviors we are not arguing that related behaviors within a period are unimportant but that the selected task or behavior is a good representation of the construct during the particular period.

The idea of social tasks or marker behaviors is consistent with the idea of a dominant activity originally suggested by Vygotsky and later elaborated by another Soviet psychologist, Leontiev (Lisina 1985). Within these theories "activity" refers to a child's actions and operations. If we apply the Soviet notion of dominant activity to our work, activity refers to the communication behaviors used in playing social pretend. A dominant activity is the principal one at each stage of development. The dominant activity serves to organize all types of activities. Subsequent development depends on the dominant activity (Lisina 1985).[1] Therefore, according to the Soviet theory of activity, the form of social pretend play within one period would cause the transformation that results in the form of social pretend play in the subsequent period. Specifically, because children have mastered the communication of meaning within social pretend play, they can explore issues of control and compromise by negotiating social pretend play. Likewise, children can use social pretend play to explore trust and intimacy once they have resolved issues of control and compromise in social pretend play negotiations.

We also have assumed that one activity, in this case social pretend play, can assume different developmental functions. This is possible, in part, because the activity is complex. Social pretend play even in its most rudimentary form involves the coordination of an internal world that produces nonliteral transformations with the external world of social relations (Howes et al. 1989). More complex social pretend play engages the child in counterfactual or would-be thinking as children jointly manage multiple roles, invent novel plots, and deliberately interweave pretense and reality (Bretherton 1987).

The complexity and multifunctional nature of social pretend play contributes to a somewhat confusing empirical literature on the subject. Although children's social pretend play has a rich literature, researchers infrequently make explicit their assumptions about the function of the play for children's development. Thus, social pretend play is studied as a central task of social-cognitive development (e.g., Watson & Fischer 1980), of the development of social interaction with peers (e.g., Connolly & Doyle 1984) and as emotional development (e.g., Fein 1985).

Functions of Social Pretend Play

If one is to impose an organizational structure on this literature the function of social pretend play must be defined. Bretherton (1987), in discussing the multifunctional nature of social pretend play, argues that the only social pretend function that could not be filled in other contexts is that of emotional mastery. Emotional mastery is defined as using pretend play to successfully work through fears and other emotional issues. Emotional mastery is distinct from the function of mastery of communication of meaning, and could occur in solitary pretend play as well as in social pretend play. Mastery of the communication of meaning can only occur in a social context because it is the ability to understand that nonliteral meaning can be shared and collaboratively elaborated.

Bretherton has selected a most important function for social pretend play. In contrast, in this book we will argue that social pretend play serves different functions in different periods. These two arguments are not totally incompatible. Although Bretherton acknowledges that metacommunication in pretense begins at about fifteen months, she limits her discussion of social pretend play to complex forms that involve multiple conceptual levels of representation. These forms of social pretend play emerge during preschool. In contrast, in this book we will argue that by the preschool period social pretend play serves not only the function of emotional mastery through exploring issues of intimacy and trust but that it fills other functions in earlier periods.

We have identified three functions of social pretend play. These functions are initially the communication of meaning through mastery of social pretend forms, subsequently expressing and exploring issues of control and compromise by negotiating social pretend play meanings and scripts, and finally, exploring issues of intimacy and trust within social pretend play. We suggest that each of these functions assumes greater importance within a particular developmental period. Following the argument begun by Howes we will argue that mastery of the communication of meaning in social pretend play is a central function of social pretend play in the toddler period. We will then suggest that expressing and exploring issues of control and compromise is a new and salient function of social pretend play in the early preschool period. Finally, following Gottman and Bretherton's models, we will argue that emotional mastery or exploring issues of intimacy and trust is the major function of social pretend play in older children.

By linking particular functions of social pretend play to particular age periods we do not mean to imply either a sequential model or that social pretend play has only one function within an age period. Certainly preschool children are still mastering the more subtle forms of social pretend play negotiation. Toddlers do form friendships (Howes 1983) and social pretend play between toddler-age friends may have elements of self-disclosure. Thus, toddler social pretend play may serve intimacy functions.

However, we will argue that there is a single most important function of social pretend play within a developmental period. This argument is consistent with the notion of social tasks or marker behaviors representing social competence in a particular developmental period. The argument of a single most important function is also consistent with the idea of dominant activity. Thus, social pretend play fulfills a single most important function during each developmental period. The form of social pretend play during a period contributers to the reorganization of the form in the next period. The particular function of social pretend play is closely tied to the demands for social competence within each period. The demands for social competence are, in turn, determined by the social, cognitive, and linguistic skills of the child and the increasingly complex social contexts for development.

In discussing the changing functions of social pretend play we are assuming that as the child moves from the toddler to the preschool stages of development he or she is in contact for longer and longer periods with an increasingly varied peer group. This assumption is true for children enrolled in child care. With age the number of children in the child-care peer group increases while the amount of adults provided for each child decreases. For children living in more traditional families the transition between toddler and preschool periods is usually marked by either enrollment in a formal preschool program or increasing amounts of time in the informal neighborhood peer group.

The Partner in Social Pretend Play

In our organizational scheme it is important to consider characteristics of the social pretend play partner in order to understand the changing functions of social pretend play. Social pretend play by definition is a social rather than individual activity. It is impossible to generate social pretend play without a partner. The function of this play is influenced, as we shall discuss, by the nature of the available partner. For example, adult-child social pretend play differs in features and, we will argue, function, from peer social pretend play.

The literature on pretend as opposed to social pretend play is composed of studies in five different partner contexts: child alone or with an adult who elicits but does not join in play; mother-child pretend play; sibling pretend play; and pretend play between age-mates. There is an implicit organization by age within these studies. Studies of solitary pretend play and mother-child pretend play rarely extend to preschoolers. Studies of sibling pretend play cluster in the toddler period. Studies of social pretend play between peers are most common with preschool-age children. In discussing the functions of social pretend play we will limit ourselves to the four dyadic partner contexts. We will not consider solitary or elicited pretend play. We also will not consider large group social pretend play. Children younger than four or five rarely engage in social pretend play in groups larger than two or three. Even with the older preschoolers, when six or seven children may be in the game most interactive play occurs within dyads. We will also not consider adult-elicited or play-training or tutoring pretend play. There is excellent literature on this topic initiated by a pioneering study by Smilansky (1968) but it is beyond the scope of this book (see Johnson et al. 1987 for a review).

The function of social pretend play assumed by the researcher predetermines the age of the play partner. If the researcher is primarily interested in the mastery function of social pretend play then studies of the transmission of the culture of play from expert (mother or older sibling) to the novice (the toddler-age child) are especially interesting. Children who are mastering the communication of meaning in social pretend play can use the scaffold provided by a partner who has mastered this play device. As we shall see, mothers and siblings often provide a structure for the play and coach the younger child in playing techniques.

Studies of mother-child pretend play drop out about the time that theme and script negotiation assume greatest importance in social pretend play. We suspect that pretend play becomes less interesting and enjoyable for mothers who are probably engaged in multiple real-life arguments with the child. For the child, pretend play with siblings and peers may be a safer avenue for exploring control and compromise than pretend play with the more powerful adults.

If a researcher is concerned with the self-disclosure function of social pretend play, then studies of same-age peers, particularly of friend partners, are interesting. Studies of social pretend play with peers increase at a time when friendship is a central concern for children (Corsaro 1985; Parker & Gottman 1989). Issues of intimacy and trust are central to friendships and, as will be discussed, children's friendships and their pretend play are also interrelated.

The nature of the play partner-child relationship as well as the age of the partner are relevant in defining functions of social pretend play. If the function of social pretend play is to master communication of meaning then we might assume that mastery will be more complete if the play partner is sensitive and responsive to the child's attempts to communicate. Therefore, children with secure attachments might be expected to excel at social pretend play because secure attachments are formed from experiences with a sensitive and responsive partner. Several studies do report a link between the child's attachment relationship with the mother and the child's symbolic play with both the mother and with peers (Bretherton et al. 1979; Matas, Arend, & Sroufe 1978; Slade 1987a). Similarly, children with siblings who were particularly skillful at eliciting and responding to beginning attempts to communicate pretend might master social pretend play before children with no siblings or less sensitive siblings. Therefore, the nature of the sibling-child relationship might be expected to influence the quality of sibling-child play (Furman & Buhrmester 1985) although there are no studies that directly address this issue.

Friendships, particularly friendships that are especially close and/or stable, might be expected to influence both the exploration of control and compromise and the intimacy and trust functions of social pretend play. Gottman (1986) reports that preschool friends have more harmonious play than acquaintances. We suspect that this relation between friends and the ability to negotiate play would also be true during the toddler period. Later in the preschool period children who are friends may use social pretend play to explore their fears, achieve trust, and for intimacy functions. Children who do not have friends or are less well adjusted may have more difficulty with this function of social pretend play. Several studies report differences in social pretend play between friends and acquaintances (Gottman & Parkhurst

1980; Howes & Unger 1989; Roopnarine & Field 1984). We will examine these studies for differences in the use of social pretend play.

Summary

Social pretend play is considered a marker of social competence in two recent models of the development of social relationships and social competence. Although these models appear, at first, to have used social pretend play in contradictory ways, we suggest that the models are compatible if the functions of social pretend play are assumed to change with development. We propose three different functions of social pretend play during childhood. During the earliest period of social pretend play the function of the play is to master the communication of meaning. As children develop sufficient linguistic and cognitive skills to engage in social pretend play negotiations, we see the function of social pretend play changing. The function of the play becomes exploring issues of control and compromise through negotiation. Finally, once children become expert players of social pretend we see the function of social pretend as exploring issues of trust and intimacy.

We further suggest that the social pretend play partner is important in understanding the functions of social pretend play. Mastery functions are enhanced by more expert partners and by partners who are sensitive to the child's attempts to communicate. Harmonious negotiations and intimacy and trust functions are influenced by the relationships between play partners. Children who are friends may be more likely to successfully resolve issues of autonomy and control and to use social pretend play to explore intimacy and trust.

Much of the research on social pretend play is descriptive. We have taken an inductive approach to this material, using the descriptions of play to support our notions of the functions of social pretend play and to generate a set of generalizations and hypotheses useful to future research.

About this Book

This book is a product of a research group in the Developmental Studies Program at the University of California at Los Angeles. We met weekly from the winter of 1986 through the summer of 1989 to discuss the interrelations among the development of early peer relations and social pretend play. The central ideas of the book and the research agenda suggested were generated through discussions among the group participants, Carollee Howes, and her graduate students who author or coauthor sections of the book. The book is organized according to social pretend play functions: mastering the communication of meaning, exploring control and compromise, and expressing intimacy and trust. Each section begins with a review chapter written by Carollee Howes, in collaboration with Olivia Unger and Catherine Matheson. These review chapters describe the function of social pretend play and explore the significance of both the play partner's age and the child's relationship with the partner for social pretend play within the period. The review chapters are followed by several illustrative studies. These illustrative studies, not published elsewhere, are original designs suggested by the review chapters. They were designed to elaborate productive research directions. We hope that the book will encourage other researchers to work in this area and to continue to elaborate the developmental functions of social pretend play.

Part I

MASTERY OF THE COMMUNICATION OF MEANING

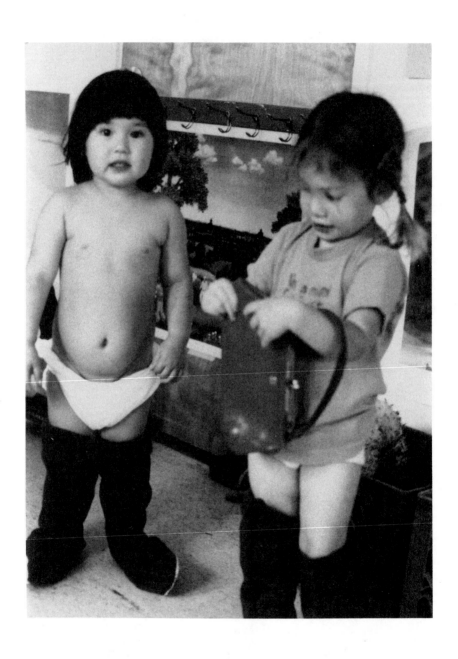

2

Mastery of the Communication of Meaning in Social Pretend Play

According to the Howes (1987, 1988) model of the development of social competence with peers, the central social task for two- to three-year-old children is mastering the communication of meaning. For younger children, peer play occurs within a complementary and reciprocal structure. The children's actions and the nature of the game (e.g., run-chase), permit children to play cooperatively without communicating meaning. Once children have the symbolic function they can communicate meaning, (e.g., naming a game, "Let's play horsies," or playing pretend). We believe the function of social pretend play within this early period is the mastery of the communication of meaning, particularly nonliteral meaning, within the play context.

There are several requirements to playing even simple pretend with a partner. Both partners must agree to play with each other. They must understand that meaning can be nonliteral as well as literal and that nonliteral meanings may be shared. And each partner must let the other know which actions and statements have nonliteral meaning. Mastering social pretend skills appears to occur in a sequential fashion. When the play partners are peers and, thus, both novices at play, social pretend play appears to develop through progressively more complex integration of pretense and social play (Howes 1985; Howes et al. 1989). When the play partner is an expert the child appears to become a progressively active participant within the play structure provided by the expert partner.

Because children usually enjoy playing pretend, it is a frequent activity during this period. Through repeated experiences of social pretend play children become increasingly successful in communicating meaning with novice as well as expert players. Therefore, these successive games of social pretend play function to enhance their communication of meaning.

There are probably multiple determinants of the emergence of social pretend play forms between approximately fifteen months and three years. In general, this is a transitional period in development with major qualitative shifts in both cognitive and language development. Furthermore, in its earliest period social pretend play is most often played with adult or older child partners rather than peer partners. Therefore, to understand the function of mastering communication of meaning within social pretend play we must examine changes in both cognitive and language development and in the structuring role of the older partner.

A search of the literature on social pretend play forms in children between fifteen months and three years yielded twelve descriptive studies. We organized these studies by age and partner. The age periods selected correspond to those used by Howes et al. (1989) to describe the emergence of social pretend play forms with peer partners. The partner categories we selected were adults, usually mothers, older siblings, and peers. We defined peers as children within six months of the same age. Descriptive accounts in the studies were used to characterize social pretend play by age period and partner. These descriptions are presented in table 2.1.

Sequential Forms of Social Pretend Play

In its earliest form, social pretend play consists of the child performing a pretend action outside of the context of joint play but in the presence of a partner. This behavior emerges at about twelve to fifteen months. See table 2.1. Research on solitary pretend play suggests that during the same period children perform autosymbolic pretend acts that are familiar, outside of the act's usual context, and directed to the self (Bretherton 1984; Fein 1981; Fenson 1984; Fenson & Ramsay 1980; Largo & Howard 1979a, 1979b; Lezine 1973; Lowe 1975; McCune-Nicolich 1981; Nicolich 1977; Watson & Fischer 1977; 1980; Wolf 1982). For example, a child may pretend to drink from an empty cup. Since the child cannot direct the pretend act to a partner but only to the self, social pretend play is constrained by the child's capacity for pretend.

Characteristics of the play partner determine whether these earliest pretend actions communicate social meaning. An adult social partner, through comments, suggestions, or demonstrations, may give the child's isolated and autosymbolic pretend act social meaning. For example, a mother might respond to a child's pretend drinking from a cup by saying "Oh, we are having a tea party," pretending to drink from her empty cup, and demonstrating

Table 2.1 Mastery of the Communication of Meaning in Social Pretend Play

ADULT	OLDER SIB	PEER
Age Period		
12–15 months		
Mother structures child's actions by commenting, suggesting, and demonstrating. The child is corrected when her pretend acts violate the real world.[a]		Isolated pretend acts within social play do not elicit a response but children watch and imitate the partner's pretend.[b]
16–20 months		
Mother structures child's actions by commenting, suggesting, and demonstrating. The child is corrected when her pretend acts violate the real world. The child imitates, watches, and complies with the mother.[c]	Sib directs, corrects, describes, names, or labels objects as well as prohibits child's acts. Child complies, imitates, and watches the sib.[d]	Children engage in similar or identical pretend acts. Children attempt to recruit the partner to joint pretend.[b]
21–24 months		
Mother becomes an interested spectator who creates a context and provides support for the child's enactments.[e]	Child and sib are complementary actors in joint role enactment and joint role play.[f]	Children engage in similar pretend actions while they simultaneously engage in social exchange. Children join the pretend of the partner, attempt to recruit the partner to joint play, and organize materials for joint pretend.[b]
25–30 months		
Child offers storyline or script. Mother requests creation of new elements and prompts child to a more realistic or detailed enactment.[g]		Each partner's pretend reflects the same script but their actions show no within pair integration. Partners inform each other of the script by

Table 2.1   *(continued)*

ADULT	OLDER SIB	PEER
25–30 months *(cont.)*		comments on their own pretend and telling the other how to act.[h]
31–36 months		
Mother praises and encourages indepen-dence. May pretend with child.[i]	Joint development of play and joint role play.[j]	Joint pretend with enact-ment of complementary roles. Children discrimi-nate between speech used for enactment and speech about enactment. Chil-dren assign roles and negotiate pretend themes and plans.[k]

[a] DeLoache & Plaetzer 1985; Kavanaugh, Whittington, & Cerbone 1983.
[b] Howes 1985; Howes & Unger 1989; Howes et al. 1989.
[c] DeLoache & Plaetzer 1985; Fiese 1988; Kavanaugh et al. 1983; O'Connell & Bretherton 1984; Farver 1989.
[d] Farver 1989.
[e] DeLoache & Plaetzer 1985; Dunn & Dale 1984; Farver 1989; Miller & Garvey 1984; Fiese 1989.
[f] Dunn & Dale 1984; Farver 1989.
[g] DeLoach & Plaetzer 1985; Kavanaugh et al. 1983; Miller & Garvey 1984; O'Connell & Bretherton 1984.
[h] Garvey 1982; Howes et al. 1989; Miller & Garvey 1984; Sachs, Goldman, & Chaille 1984.
[i] Farver 1989; Fiese 1988, 1989.
[j] Farver 1989.
[k] Forys & McCune-Nicolich 1984; Garvey 1982; Garvey & Berndt 1977; Goncu 1987; Howes 1985; Howes & Unger 1989; Howes et al. 1989; Iwanaga 1973.

how to eat pretend cookies. A peer does not have either the pretend or the social communicative capacities to create social meaning. However, because the child's pretend act is interesting and because the partner has newly emerged abilities to create autosymbolic acts, a peer partner may watch and imitate the pretend act.

Therefore, the earliest forms of social pretend play function to commu-nicate meaning only if a partner assigns meaning to the act. Through experiences of having social meaning assigned to one's pretend acts by an expert partner, the child may begin to understand that the meaning of pretend acts may be communicated to the partner. If the partner is a peer and shows interest in an act in which no meaning is assigned, the child may begin to understand that pretend acts have social value. Early peer interaction is extremely fragile and subject to disruption. Therefore, an action that elicits a peer response is likely to be recognized as one that sustains interaction and to be repeated.

By sixteen to twenty months children perform decentered symbolic games in solitary pretend (Bretherton 1984; Fein 1979; 1981; Fenson 1984; Fenson & Ramsay 1980; Largo & Howard 1979a, 1979b; Lezine 1973; Lowe 1975; McCune-Nicolich 1981; Nicolich 1977; Watson & Fischer 1977; 1980; Wolfe 1982). In decentered symbolic games children's pretend acts are performed on objects and are more abstracted and distanced from their sensorimotor actions. The child's increased capacity for pretend is reflected in social pretend play as seen in table 2.1. The child now responds to the expert (mother or sibling) player's structuring of the social play by imitating, complying, or protesting the other's play suggestions. For example, Darren, age eighteen months, was playing with his older brother, Robert, age four. Each child had a stuffed foot-high horse. Robert was carefully holding a doll on top of the horse and putting the horse through a series of maneuvers typical of a horse show. Darren sat on top of the horse and "galloped" across the room much as Robert had made the horse behave with the doll. Robert said "No, Darren, the dolls ride the horses." Darren said, "No, me ride horsie."

Within peer social pretend play the children match their pretend acts so that each child performs the same act simultaneously and children attempt to recruit the partner to join their pretend. For example, Jennifer, age eighteen months and Josh, age nineteen months, are side by side in the playroom. Jennifer picks up a toy car and runs it along the floor making motor noises. She looks at Josh and holds out the car to him. He picks up a bright red truck and moves it along the floor making similar noises. Social pretend play becomes more possible because the child is no longer limited to pretend acts directed to the self. The child appears to recognize that the partner can also pretend. On the other hand, the child's capacity both to pretend and to engage in social play with peers is still limited and the coordination of both social exchanges and common pretend activities appears beyond the child's ability (Howes et al. 1989).

We believe that when children match social pretend acts to the acts of their peers or add their own pretend suggestions to those of the expert player, they are beginning to understand that meaning can be communicated within social pretend play. At this point they appear to understand that nonliteral meanings can be shared by partners. They also appear to distinguish between literal and nonliteral meaning and to use nonliteral meaning to extend and expand the play. By this second phase in its development, social pretend play is functioning to enhance mastery of the communication of meaning. The meaning being communicated is still very simple but children are creating variations in their play. These variations extend the play and make it a truly dyadic activity.

By the end of the second year, social pretend play with both peers and expert players has become coordinated. Pretend actions are now embedded within a social play context. See table 2.1. For example, Geoff, twenty-six months, and Ginny, twenty-seven months, are in the housekeeping corner at the child-care center. Geoff is setting the table with cups. Ginny turns away from the stove where she has been cooking. "Time to eat," she says. Geoff sits down at the table and smiles at Ginny. He lifts his cup and pretends to drink. Ginny carries a pot from the stove to the table.

Ellen, twenty-five months, and Wally, her older brother, age five, are playing at their pretend stove and table as their father cooks dinner. Wally tells Ellen that she is the baby, she must sit in the chair and he will get her dinner. Wally says, "Here is your bottle and some mashed peas, baby. Eat your dinner, baby." Ellen smiles and pretends to eat. Wally offers an empty bowl and says, "Now here is your mashed elephant, baby. Eat your dinner, baby." Ellen giggles and pretends to eat. The father says, "Oh, what good children, here is your mashed dragon. Eat your dinner, children," and pretends to hand each of them a bowl. Both children giggle and pretend to eat from the bowl.

We suggest that coordinated social pretend play is possible in part because of changes in cognitive capacities. Research in solitary pretend play suggests that at about twenty to twenty-four months children begin to both sequence pretend acts and to attribute active or independent agency to inanimate objects (Bretherton et al. 1979; Bretherton et al. 1984; Brownell 1986; Fenson 1984; Fenson & Ramsay 1980; Jackowitz & Watson 1980; Largo & Howard 1979a, 1979b; Lezine 1973; Lowe 1975; McCune-Nicolich 1981; Nicolich 1977; O'Connell & Gerard 1985; Watson & Fischer 1977; Wolfe 1982). If a child can attribute active agency to an inanimate object certainly she can attribute active agency to a play partner. At this point the child appears to realize that pretend is an activity that can be shared with a social partner, that is, both partners can play the pretending game. See illustrative study #2.

Once children appear to understand that pretend can be shared, the nature of the partner appears to determine the sophistication of the resulting social pretend play. Play with age-mates is very simple. Children are playing together but there is little or no joint organization of the pretend. In contrast, when a child plays with an older sibling the children may engage in joint role enactment and role play. The younger child appears as a willing and somewhat capable participant but the older child supplies the necessary coordination of the play. Likewise, in mother-child social pretend play, the mother is still primarily responsible for creating the shared context of pretending. See illustrative study #1. From this stage onward in the development of progressively more complex social pretend play forms, each instance of social pretend play functions to provide the children with experiences in the communication of meaning.

Social and solitary pretend play between peers in children younger than twenty-five to thirty months of age lacks a script. Scripted peer social pretend play emerges by thirty months. See table 2.1. A script is a rudimentary story line understood by both partners and serving to structure and communicate the pretend play meaning (Nelson & Seidman 1984). In solitary pretend play between twenty-five and thirty months, the child begins to internally generate games with a hierarchical structure (McCune-Nicolich 1981; O'Connell & Gerard 1985). The same underlying cognitive structures that permit the creation of hierarchically structured games in solitary pretend may also contribute to the creation of scripts in social pretend play.

By twenty-five to thirty months, children devise social pretend play scripts with both experts and novices. With both partners early scripts are based on familiar everyday events such as cooking or shopping (Bretherton 1984; Gearhart 1983; Nelson & Seidman 1984). However, the use of scripts appears quite different depending on the partner. With mothers, the child devises the script and the mother appears to check it for accuracy or to press for elaboration. In contrast, within peer social pretend the script is jointly determined by the partners. The partner is kept informed and may be told how to act out the pretend but there is no authority for the correct way to act out the script.

Many early social pretend play scripts are not verbally articulated. The story line develops as a series of linked pretend actions. However, it is within the twenty-five to thirty-month period that children begin to provide a verbal script for the play. Scripts are often one of the first experiences a child has in verbally communicating meaning to a peer.

The identity of the partner may begin to assume greater importance in social pretend with peers during this period. Because the communication of meaning and social communication skills are still fairly basic both partners must know the script before they can play. Children do not yet negotiate or sometimes even name the script, they simply both play the game (e.g., feeding or rocking the babies). We expect children with a history of common experiences will be better able to engage in early scripted social pretend than unacquainted children or children with different social histories.

By thirty-one to thirty-six months children's social pretend play is shaped by the children's increasing awareness of social roles (Howes et al. 1989). Children may assign roles in play and they enact complementary roles. See table 2.1. Children must perceive the self as distinct from the other in order to enact a social role. Therefore, the ability to enact social roles is assumed to be predicated on the child's ability to decenter actions from the self (Watson & Fischer 1980). By age three children demonstrate their ability to decenter in solitary play by attributing active agency to inanimate objects and object substitutions (Fein 1979; Largo & Howard 1979a, 1979b; McCune-Nicolich 1981; Nicolich 1977; Watson & Fischer 1977).

By the time children are three they have mastered the basic elements of social pretend play. They understand that nonliteral meaning can be shared and they can successfully and completely integrate pretend actions into complex social play. They have mastered the communication of meaning within social pretend play and once this is accomplished they can use social pretend to serve other functions. Play as a way to explore issues of control and compromise and of intimacy and trust is now possible.

Much of the preceding section has focused on interactions between cognitive achievements internal to the child that make possible the production of subsequently more complex social pretend play forms and the response of the play partner to these play initiatives. More complex forms of play emerge as the child develops more sophisticated symbolic representation and social communicative skills. At this point in our discussion we will change the focus from developments centered within the child to factors within the social environment that may facilitate the mastery of play forms.

Other- to Self-Regulated Play

The sequence of pretend play forms with the mother, and to some extent older siblings shown in table 2.1, can be considered a sequence from other to self-regulated social pretend play. See illustrative study #1. The terms "other-regulation" and "self-regulation" (Wertsch 1979) are derived from the work of Vygotsky and Bruner. The term "other-regulation" refers to the performance by another person of behaviors that assist the child in the performance of a particular task. Within other regulation the adult provides a context for the child and this context permits the child to assume "self" regulation of the behavior. In Bruner's words the adult provides a social scaffold in which the adult's behavior is predictable (Bruner 1978). Children can then develop "on their own" within this framework. Within social pretend play, mothers initially (the first two age periods in table 2.1) provide other-regulation by commenting on, suggesting, and demonstrating pretend play. Later (the third, fourth, and fifth age periods in table 2.1), when the child is self-regulating pretend play, mothers are less active in play, primarily providing a supportive context and secondarily taking the other-regulation role by asking the child to elaborate his or her play.

Initially mother-child and sibling-child social pretend play appears more sophisticated than peer-peer play. This increased sophistication is probably due to the other-regulation of the play by the more experienced player. By structuring play in the child's zone of proximal development (Vygotsky 1978), the child can participate in more complex play than he or she can generate with age-mates. In this case the zone of proximal development includes play just slightly more complex than the child can produce on his/her own. Once the child can produce sophisticated social pretend on his/her own, social pretend play with age-mates is generally more complex than adult-child social pretend. In the next section of this review we will suggest that this shift has less to do with the capacities of the adult player for social pretend than with the changing functions of social pretend play and the willingness of the adult to engage in play.

The communication of meaning is more difficult with peer partners than when the partner is an expert. We suggest, however, that play with both types of partners is important in the mastering of the communication of meaning. Mothers and siblings will attribute meaning to a child's pretend actions. They will also fill in and expand the meaning of a younger child's action. For example, when a toddler makes a roaring type noise she may or may not be pretending to be a tiger and certainly she is not suggesting an elaborate hunting, chasing, and catching game with a single roar. However, a preschool-age sibling might build on the roar by script production, "I'm going to find that tiger and make tiger stew for dinner," and pretend actions such as creeping up on the "tiger," pretending to tie up the "tiger," or putting the "tiger" in the "stewpot." We suggest that it is through participating in this activity structure that the younger child understands and masters the communication of meaning and the concept of scripts.

A peer is initially less likely than an expert player partner to attribute meaning or to expand and extend the pretend action of the partner into an elaborated social pretend play sequence. The toddler's roar would be more likely to be matched by another roar than expanded into a game. However, as we have discussed, because the partner's pretend act is interesting the peer will try to incorporate it into the social play of the dyad. Both "tigers" might roar and simultaneously be involved in a run-chase game. Repeated efforts to share and coordinate nonliteral meanings with peer partners combined with the development of more sophisticated cognitive, social, and linguistic skills function to provide the child with more and more complex social pretend play experiences. Pretend and social play become truly integrated so that only the roaring partner will chase while the partner pretends to be frightened by the roaring "tiger". Through these experiences within social pretend play the child masters the communication of meaning.

Affective Relationships with Play Partners—Adults

The harmoniousness of the caregiver-child relationship is associated with the emergence of pretend play. More harmonious dyads, and dyads with greater maternal involvement, are associated with higher levels of pretend play (Adler & McCune 1985; Bretherton et al. 1979; Dunn & Wooding 1979; O'Connell & Bretherton 1984; Slade 1987a). Attachment theory suggests an explanation for this link between the quality of maternal involvement and the child's use of symbols. Children's freedom to explore their environment as well as their competence in such explorations are directly related to their expectations that the caregiver will meet their need for comfort and nurturing (Ainsworth et al. 1978). Children rated as more secure with their mothers are also more advanced in symbolic play (Belsky 1984; Bretherton et al. 1979; Matas et al. 1978; Slade 1987a). Only one study to date has examined differences in the ways mothers of secure and anxious children involve themselves in play (Slade 1987a). In the Slade study, children classified as secure in the Ainsworth Strange Situation (Ainsworth et al. 1978) were more competent in social pretend when playing with their mothers than when they were playing alone. In contrast, the play of children classified as anxious was not enhanced by play with the mother. It appears that either the mothers of anxiously attached children were unable to provide a scaffold for the play attempts of the children or that the anxious children were unable to use the other regulation provided by the mother.

Secure maternal attachments are associated with sensitive caregiving (Belsky 1983). We suspect that sensitive caregiving is implicated in the mastery of the communication of meaning function of social pretend play. If children are to master the communication of meaning within social pretend play within adult-child pretend play, the children's attempts to communicate meaning must receive sensitive responses. We can imagine mother-child social pretend play in which a talented mother puts on an exciting pretend show for the child but rejects or ignores the child's play variation and suggestions, and/or intrudes upon the child's own attempts to formulate play. Highly directive adult partners play pretend through a series of directives (e.g., "Make the cow say moo," "Put the cow in the barn," "Make the horse say neigh," "Put the horse in the wagon"). We doubt that this type of adult-child play is as effective in helping the child to master the communication of meaning than adult-child play that involves more sensitive listening to and expanding on the child's self-initiated play. In support of this expectation, Unger and Howes (1988) studied mother-toddler social pretend play and found that monitoring and structuring the child's ongoing activity enhanced the complexity of the play while setting up play activities and altering the play situation did not. Likewise, Fiese (1989) reports that maternal intrusiveness or watching in mother-toddler pretend play led to exploratory play while the mother's turn taking and more reciprocal forms of interaction led to symbolic play.

Peers

The affective relationship between the peer and the child as well as between the child and the mother may also influence the mastery of social pretend play forms. As discussed earlier if the earliest social pretend play scripts are based on familiar everyday occurrences, friends are most likely to have a reservoir of shared occurrences to use in developing scripts. Toddler-age friends engage in more complex social play than acquaintances (Howes 1983). The increased complexity of play between friends appears based on the nature of early toddler interaction. Because these children are limited in their ability to communicate with language, their play is often built on well-learned routine and ritual-like games (Howes 1988). These games are developed jointly over time between stable peer partners. Friends are defined as children who chose each other as interactive partners and who enjoy each other's company (Howes 1988). Friends, therefore, may be most likely to explore and perfect social pretend play. The well-rehearsed structure of play between friends may serve to attribute and expand the communication of meaning in a manner similar to adult-child social pretend play. In social pretend play between peers the toddler "roar" may connote an integrated run-and-chase game with the tiger chasing and the partner running. This integration is possible because of the shared experience of run-and-chase games and role reversals. Friends do not have to simultaneously devise the game structure and integrate or communicate the pretend meanings. Instead, they integrate pretend meanings into well-developed and routinelike games structures. A small pilot study (Howes & Unger 1989) supports these conclusions. Children identified as friends engaged in more social pretend play at earlier ages than acquaintances.

Summary

In summary, we have argued that the function of social pretend play from approximately three to thirty-six months is the mastery of the communication of meaning. As social pretend play becomes possible due to increases in cognitive and linguistic capacities, children engage in pretend play with mothers, older siblings, and peers. The ability of the child to communicate meaning and to engage in pretend play appears to influence the researchers' choice of partner. The mother is the preferred partner in the majority of the studies of the youngest children while age-mate studies predominate as the children grow older. The age of the partner is linked to the child's competence as a pretend player. During the earliest period, the scaffold provided by the mother or the older sibling increases the child's ability to engage in more complex social pretend. As the child becomes able to self-regulate pretend, the social pretend play of peers becomes more complex. Finally, we have suggested that the nature of the affective relationship with the mother and with the peer influences the complexity of the child's social pretend play. The illustrative studies following this review elaborate on existing knowledge of children mastering the communication of meaning by exploring the processes and strategies underlying successful early social pretend play. The first study, "Mothers and Toddlers: Partners in Early Symbolic Play," first compares children's solitary play and their social pretend play with their mothers as partner. The study goes on to ask what makes mothers successful play partners? Three theoretical models for mother-child social pretend are reviewed and mother-child interaction around pretend play objects is described. How well each model fits the observed mother-child interaction is discussed. The second study, "Collaborative Construction of Social Pretend Play between Toddler-Age Partners," explores the differing efficacy of toddler's social pretend play strategies. Toddler strategies are evaluated in terms of the extent to which the child is able to adjust his or her behavior to the behavior of a partner. In this study we explored the assumption that adjusting one's behavior indicates that the child understands that pretend meanings can be social.

A persistent debate in the pretend play literature revolves around socioeconomic and cultural differences in children's play. Initially, this debate was framed in the deficit model. Children from low-income homes (Smilansky 1968) or from less technologically and economically advanced societies (Schwartzman 1978) were assumed to be less imaginative than children from more advantaged homes and societies. Further research suggests that while there may be group differences among children of different backgrounds there are not necessarily competency differences (McLoyd 1980). (See Johnson et al. (1987) for a review and excellent discussion of these issues.) Most of the research on SES and cultural differences in social pretend play have looked at social pretend play as a product or outcome rather than examining processes within the play. Our third illustrative study, "An Analysis of Young American and Mexican Children's Play Dialogues," is an exception to this trend. In this study we describe play negotiation styles in children from very different cultures.

3

Mothers and Toddlers: Partners in Early Symbolic Play: Illustrative Study #1

Laura Beizer and Carollee Howes

While an extensive body of research exists to document the development of toddlers' independent symbolic play (e.g., Fein 1981; Fenson et al. 1976; Fenson 1984; Largo & Howard 1979a, 1979b; Lowe 1975; Nicolich 1977), relatively less is known about how symbolic play develops in a social context. The current study compared toddlers' independent symbolic play with collaborative symbolic play between toddlers and mothers. The study also examined the nature of the mothers' contributions to their toddlers' early symbolic play endeavors. While a growing body of research suggests that adults *do* influence toddlers' play, the nature and impact of such adult input is not yet fully understood.

Independent and Collaborative Symbolic Play

Several recent studies have compared toddlers' independent symbolic play with collaborative symbolic play between mothers and toddlers (DeLoache & Plaetzer 1985; Fiese 1989, 1990; O'Connell & Bretherton 1984; Miller & Garvey 1984). In general, these studies conclude that toddlers engage in both quantitatively and qualitatively more diverse and advanced forms of symbolic play when playing with mothers than when playing alone. However, researchers know more about the finding that adults seem to enhance toddlers' emerging pretend capacities than how or why this occurs.

Although neither DeLoache and Plaetzer (1985) nor Fiese (1990) explicitly tested the impact of different types of input on toddlers' symbolic play, their research provides some insight into the mechanisms that may assist toddlers during collaborative play with their mothers. While DeLoache and Fiese do not directly discuss the impact of maternal input on toddlers' symbolic play, they have suggested various forms that maternal input might take. Specifically, these researchers identified the following forms of maternal assistance that occurred during symbolic play between mothers and toddlers: *physical attention, directing, and/or assistance* (Fiese 1989, 1990; DeLoache & Plaetzer 1985), *questioning, instructing* (Fiese 1989, 1990) and/or *correcting* (DeLoache & Plaetzer 1985), *naming, labeling* (Fiese 1989, 1990), and *verbal elaboration* (DeLoache & Plaetzer 1985); *direct maternal suggestions* (DeLoache & Plaetzer 1985).

In addition, Fiese compared toddlers' independent pretend play with their free play with mothers, play during a modeling condition, and play following the modeling condition. Fiese found that toddlers engaged in the most complex forms of play when their mothers encouraged them to imitate several pretend activities during the modeling condition. This finding suggests that mothers might assist toddlers by modeling symbolic play acts, and that modeling could help explain the common finding that toddlers engage in more complex symbolic play when playing with mothers than when playing alone. However, Fiese's finding occurred in, and is therefore limited to, symbolic play in experimental settings. Whether mothers model symbolic play actions for their toddlers during naturally occurring play, and if so, whether modeling is more likely than other forms of maternal input to encourage toddler play, remain as important empirical questions.

Thus, extant research clearly suggests that adults facilitate toddlers' symbolic play, but only eludes to the ways in which such assistance may occur. The following brief discussion of models concerned with adult assistance of a child's cognitive performance is now presented to suggest the value of formulating similar models to investigate adult input into the development of symbolic play.

Theoretical Models: Adult Input and Cognitive Development

Both theory and extant research suggest the importance of adults as facilitators of a child's early cognitive development. In particular, Vygotsky's theory (Vygotsky 1962, 1978) emphasizes that *all* cognitive development is mediated by social factors, and suggests that developmental changes in a child's cognitive capacities occur first in the context of social interaction with skilled partners, and are only later internalized and manifested by children in their independent activities. Vygotsky further suggests that adults' input into children's cognitive development is maximized when adults concentrate their assistance at just above the level at which children can accomplish independently. Thus, adults help children to accomplish with assistance what they cannot yet accomplish on their own by acting within the child's "zone of proximal development"—the difference between what children can accomplish independently and with adult assistance.

Researchers have most often studied the impact of adult guidance on children's tasks performance during puzzle (Wertsch 1979; Wertsch et al. 1980; Wood 1976), and counting activities (Saxe, Gearhart, & Guberman 1984; Saxe 1987). Generally, results of these studies suggest that adults "fine-tune" their assistance to match or slightly exceed the level at which children are able to perform independently, and systematically adjust their assistance in an appropriate hierarchical manner as children succeed or fail. Thus, these studies suggest that adults act within children's zones of proximal development to facilitate children's task performance, at least during certain types of joint activity.

Studies of adult assistance of children's performance in the zone of proximal development have typically focused on problem-solving activities. Within these activities, an explicit goal is generally specified, and a particular outcome is considered correct.

Less is known about the ways in which adults assist infants during play, an activity that is inherently different from more structured problem-solving tasks. In contrast with puzzle or counting activities, play is relatively unstructured. Play activities rarely focus on achieving one particular goal, and instead, allow an unlimited number of alternatives, each of which may be considered correct, or at least acceptable. Consequently, one might expect the nature of adults' interactions with children during symbolic play and the ways in which such interactions assist children's play performance to differ from the ways in which adults help children to solve problems and puzzle tasks. Whereas one might reasonably expect adults to modify their behavior in an ordered fashion in response to a child's attempts to solve a specified puzzle or counting task, expecting parents to follow a certain sequence in the level of their play suggestions when pretending with toddlers may be inconsistent with the nature of play activity.

Because the differences between play and more goal-directed, problem-solving activities might suggest different patterns of adult input into children's performances, the current study proposed and assessed several alternative models of adult contributions to toddlers' emerging capacities for symbolic play. These models were derived from Vygotsky's general theory of socially mediated cognitive development, research based on Vygotsky's theory to study adult-assisted performance in children's problem-solving and number activities, and in particular, the concepts of the "zone of proximal development" and "scaffolding," as well as a review of research concerned with toddlers' social and symbolic play with adults.

Proposed Models: Adult Input Into Symbolic Play

The "zone of proximal development" model. The first model, referred to in this chapter as the zone of proximal development position, suggests that adults fine-tune their input into play to match toddlers' emerging symbolic play capacities in a manner similar to that demonstrated by in studies of children's adult-assisted performances on problem-solving and counting tasks. According to this position, adults assist toddlers in their zones of proximal development—such as making suggestions for symbolic play at levels just above the level of pretend play toddlers can accomplish independently.

A few studies indirectly suggest that a zone of proximal development model might accurately describe adults' input into toddler symbolic play. In the context of these studies, adults verbally suggested and/or modeled pretend activities at levels beyond the toddlers' observed, independent play capacity. These pretend suggestions elicited higher levels of pretend play from toddlers than toddlers exhibited independently and spontaneously (Belsky & Most 1984; Fiese 1989; Fenson 1984; Fenson et al. 1976; Watson & Fischer 1977). While results of these studies suggest that adults may act as scaffolds for toddlers' symbolic play, these results are limited to analyses of experimentally elicited pretend, and do not explore the nature and impact of adults' roles in naturally occurring episodes of collaborative symbolic play.

The "smorgasbord" model. The previous review of modeling studies suggests the relevance of a zone of proximal development position for a model of adult input into symbolic play. Simultaneously, the limitations of these studies to experimental settings, and the less-structured and goal-directed nature of naturally occurring play suggests that a zone of proximal development model may not accurately describe adult input into toddlers' symbolic play. O'Connell and Bretherton's work (1984) provides evidence for a second model of adult input, which is referred to in this chapter as the smorgasbord model.

Consistent with other studies of collaborative mother-toddler play, O'Connell and Bretherton found that toddlers exhibited more diverse types of symbolic play with an adult than when alone, based on an analysis of exploratory, combinatorial, and symbolic play. However, this finding was not due to the fine-tuning of pretend suggestions by adults, as a zone of proximal development model might predict. Instead, adults in this study offered the same selection of play suggestions to toddlers at all ages. At different ages, however, toddlers chose different play suggestions. O'Connell and Bretherton suggest that toddlers selected those suggestions that were most useful to them at different developmental periods.

Similar to the zone of proximal development model, the smorgasbord model proposes that adults make direct suggestions to guide toddlers' symbolic play. Unlike the zone of proximal development model, however, the smorgasbord model suggests that children, rather than adults, are responsible for selecting suggestions which approximate their zone of proximal development. While the zone of proximal development model argues that adults fine-tune their input to approximate toddlers' developing capacities, the smorgasbord position suggests that adults offer a wide variety of suggestions at a wide variety of levels, and that children select those suggestions which are most appropriate and helpful.

The "scaffolding" model. O'Connell and Bretherton's study highlights the importance of examining both adults' and children's roles in maintaining symbolic play. However, this study is limited by the assessment of only the broad category of symbolic play, rather than assessing adult and child input into symbolic play. While O'Connell and Bretherton have analyzed mothers' direct play suggestions, adults may influence toddlers' play indirectly, by mechanisms other than direct suggestion or modeling.

A third set of research studies offer insight into the nature of these mechanisms. Fiese (1989, 1990) explored some of these mechanisms and, like O'Connell and Bretherton, concluded that mothers contribute to toddler play in different ways at different ages. In contrast with O'Connell and Bretherton's findings, however, mothers, rather than toddlers, were responsible for these differences. Specifically, Fiese's mothers offered different types of input to children at different ages. Mothers were more likely to use verbally labeling techniques when playing with their two year olds than with their three year olds. Similarly, mothers were more likely to use questions and instructions when playing with their three-year-olds than their two-year-olds.

Kavanaugh, Whittington, and Cerbone (1983) and Sachs (1980) analyzed changes in the pretend language which adults addressed to developing children in the context of naturally occurring, collaborative symbolic play. Like Fiese, these researchers concluded that adults modify their input in response to the changing developmental capacities of infants and toddlers. Along with DeLoache and Plaetzer's (1985, discussed previously) and Fiese's studies, Kavanaugh et al. and Sachs's findings provide at least indirect support for a third model of adult input into toddlers' developing symbolic play, referred to in this chapter as the scaffolding model.

This model derives from research of adults as scaffolds for children's performances, as well as the previously cited studies of collaborative symbolic play. Within this framework, adults serve as temporary scaffolds, controlling "those elements of the task which are initially beyond the learner's capacity, thus permitting him to concentrate on and complete only those elements that are within his range of competence" (Wood, Bruner, & Ross 1976, 90). Within the domain of symbolic play, the scaffolding position suggests that adults assist toddlers by creating and maintaining a structure for pretend—that is, by controlling aspects of the symbolic play setting which are difficult for the novice pretender to control.

Both the scaffolding and zone of proximal development models derive from Vygotsky's theory. However, the scaffolding model suggests that mothers focus their input on teaching toddlers about pretending, and supporting the toddlers' early attempts at constructing and sharing pretend ideas, rather than targeting suggestions at particular levels of symbolic play. Thus, within the scaffolding model, adults work within the child's zone of proximal development in terms of a *general* orientation towards pretend, while adults focus on assisting children to play at specific levels of play activity within the zone of proximal development model.

Predictions and implications of proposed models. Each of these different models—zone of proximal development, smorgasbord, and scaffolding—offer different predictions about the nature and success of adult input into toddler symbolic play. The zone of proximal development model predicts that adults would concentrate their play suggestions at a level immediately above the level exhibited by children in independent play, and further, that suggestions made within this range would most successfully elicit symbolic play by toddlers. Alternately, the smorgasbord model predicts that adults would offer a wide range of play suggestions to all children, regardless of their level of development or symbolic play skill. Further, the smorgasbord model would expect the most complex symbolic play when adults' suggestions covered the widest range possible, rather than concentrating at a particular level. Finally, the scaffolding model predicts that adult input into symbolic play should focus not on making direct suggestions, but on creating and maintaining an appropriate context for pretend that supports a toddler's emerging abilities.

Whether adults follow a particular theoretical model in their interactions with toddlers during symbolic play is an empirical question. Alternately, adults may combine elements of all three models, or structure differently their input into symbolic play with toddlers as toddlers develop new skills and play in different ways. The current study explored the contributions of adults and toddlers by comparing the frequency and complexity of the toddlers' independent and collaborative symbolic play. The types, levels, and relative success of different kinds of maternal input in eliciting toddler pretend were analyzed in order to assess the validity of the zone of proximal development, smorgasbord, and scaffolding models of adult input into collaborative symbolic play.

Methods

Subjects

Subjects included six children at each of five three-month intervals between fourteen and twenty-eight months, six children at each of two five-month intervals between twenty-nine and thirty-eight months ($N = 42$), and their mothers. Age intervals were smaller prior to twenty-nine months since changes in play, as well as the pace of development in general, were expected to be most dramatic at earlier ages. Twenty children were boys and twenty-two were girls. All children were from middle- and upper-class families living in southern California.

Procedures

Toddlers were observed and videotaped in their homes during two 15-minute play sessions on the same day. In the Independent session, toddlers played without their mothers. In the Collaborative session, toddlers played with their mothers. Toddlers were first observed playing alone and then with their mothers. This decision facilitated the assessment of relations between toddlers' independent play level and maternal play suggestions in the subsequent joint play session. Clearly, this decision is accompanied by a concern regarding possible order effects. Both the value of observing, and having mothers observe, toddlers' play alone as a means of assessing maternal accommodation to toddlers' independent play abilities, and data from extant research (O'Connell & Bretherton 1984) suggest that such order effects were not intrusive and were considered valid reasons for conducting the Independent play session prior to the Collaborative play session.

Toddlers played with a standard set of toys chosen to maximize the likelihood of both pretend play and social interaction. Most toys were included in duplicate to provide a similar toy for each potential partner, thus increasing the likelihood that toddlers and adults would play together. Toys included blocks, plastic snap-together toys, a small table and two seats, and toy cups, plates, spoons, a pitcher, bottles, brushes, combs, mirrors, cars, small action figures, dolls, telephones, cradles, blankets, high chairs, and strollers.

Measures and Coding

The living room or play room of each home was cleared of the toddlers' own toys and the experimental toys were arranged in a standard order on the floor. During the Independent session, mothers were asked to remain on the side of the room or in a nearby room and to observe their children playing, but not to interfere, direct, or become involved in play. During the Collaborative session, mothers were asked to play with their children as they normally do, and to feel free to interact with their children as they would under everyday circumstances.

Independent Play Session

Generally, the first ten minutes of Independent play videotapes were selected for coding. In the event that children did not play immediately, the first ten minutes following the onset of play were selected. Pretend acts and utterances that occurred during the selected ten minutes were transcribed, and transcripts were coded for levels of the toddlers' pretend play acts and pretend utterances. Only pretend actions were analyzed in this study. Levels of child pretend actions are described in table 3.1, and were slightly modified from Fenson's pretend scales (1984).

Collaborative Play Session

Generally, the first ten minutes during the Collaborative play videotapes were selected for coding. As with the Independent session, the first ten minutes following the onset of play were selected if play did not begin immediately. Sequences of mother-toddler pretend play episodes were identified, with the end of a play episode defined by either of two types of activity. First, in cases where mothers and toddlers engaged in elaborate pretend play which revolved around a particular theme (e.g., tea party, taking care of babies, etc.), the play episode was considered to be ended if the theme changed or if play partners stopped playing at that particular time. Second, in less-sophisticated play involving isolated pretend acts that were not integrated by a theme, the pretend episode was considered over if play partners stopped playing in a pretend manner with one toy or started playing with a different toy. Sequences of mother-child pretend play episodes were transcribed, and transcripts were coded at three levels: 1) type and success of maternal input into pretend play; 2) level of maternal play suggestions; 3)

Table 3.1 Pretend Play Levels (modified from Fenson 1984)

LEVEL	DESCRIPTION	EXAMPLE (CHILD)
Self-directed	Pretend acts directed to or centered on self, or acts performed by the child in reality which in pretend use different materials, appear in different contexts, or are carried to different outcomes	Feed self with toy spoon; lie on floor with blanket as if sleeping
Passive other-directed	Same acts as in self-directed, but directed toward inanimate or animate others without attributing independent agency to other	Feed doll with bottle; push doll in stroller
Object-directed	Same acts as in self-directed, but which are directed toward nonlifelike objects	Pour from an empty toy pitcher into a cup; stir with a toy spoon in an empty toy cup
Active other-directed	Same acts as in self-directed but directed towards lifelike objects or people other than self and which attribute independent agency to objects or people	Making a doll hold a toy mirror as if looking at it's reflection; making a doll hold a bottle as if feeding itself
Single scheme sequence	Pretend acts in which the same act is directed toward two different recipients, or, first one, and then a second similar act in sequence, or two different pretend acts are performed in sequence with no logical order	Feed one doll and then a second doll; with a toy brush, stroke doll's hair first with one brush and then with a second brush; feed self with a toy spoon and then drink from an empty cup

Table 3.1 *(continued)*

LEVEL	DESCRIPTION	EXAMPLE (CHILD)
Multi-scheme sequence	Two or more pretend acts performed in sequence with a logical order	Feed a doll with a spoon and then wipe the doll's mouth with a cloth; stir with a toy spoon in an empty toy cup and then feed self with spoon
Substitution	Pretend acts in which one object is used to represent a different object	Use a toy crib as if it were a bathtub; use a block as food on a toy plate
Invent 1	Pretend acts in which an imaginary object, place, substance, or person is created or referred to, when there food from a toy is tangible contextual support, such as real objects which suggest the invention	Child pours from empty pitcher and says "coffee"; picks up imaginary plate and eats it
Invent 2	Pretend acts in which an imaginary object, place, substance, or person is created, but without tangible contextual support the invention	Child walks from one part of room to another and says, "Now I'm at the store"; child says, "Hi, Daddy," to an invisible person

form of maternal indirect input; 4) toddlers' responses to maternal play suggestions and indirect input; and 5) success of maternal suggestions and indirect input at eliciting toddler symbolic play.

Type of maternal input.   Three different types of maternal input were coded: 1) inattention; 2) indirect support; and 3) direct pretend suggestions. "Inattention" was coded when mothers were mentally and/or emotionally distracted from the toddlers' play. Thus, the only support for toddlers' play during the mothers' inattentive episodes was derived from the mothers' physical presence. Because mothers were rarely inattentive during the study (M = 1.62), the mothers' inattentive behavior was excluded from further analyses.

"Indirect support" was coded when mothers engaged in behaviors that might encourage toddlers to pretend, but only by indirect means. Thus, indirect support did not include direct suggestions for pretend or modeling of pretend acts not previously performed by the child.

Behavior codes as indirect support were next categorized as one of six types. These types included: 1) *physically assisting* the child with props that the child has arranged or is trying to arrange on his/her own, or refocusing the child's attention onto the pretend toys if he/she had strayed from them; 2) *verbalizing* the child's pretend intent, narrating the child's symbolic play activity, or labelling objects as the child uses them in pretend; 3) *elaborating* on the child's symbolic play, either by adding to or describing new elements for the child's pretend theme, joining the child to enact a pretend role similar or complementary to the role the child was playing, or relating the child's symbolic play to a real-life experience; 4) general *positive support* for the child's symbolic play, such as nodding, smiling, or positive comments; 5) offering *instruction* or demonstration of the literal (i.e., *not* symbolic) use of a prop or toy; and 6) *clarifying* the child's pretend intent or statement, either by repeating the child's comment or asking questions.

In contrast, "direct pretend suggestions" included direct verbal suggestions, instructions, or invitations to engage in particular pretend acts; gestures or modeling of specific pretend acts; or any combination of these strategies. Maternal suggestions that were coded as "direct" for type of suggestion were then also coded for the level of pretend suggested. The level of pretend implied in the mothers' direct suggestions were coded using a slightly modified version of Fenson's scale (1984) for pretend play which is summarized in table 3.1.

Success of maternal input. The percentage of maternal direct and indirect input that was successfully followed by the toddlers' performance of symbolic play acts was calculated as well. The mothers' direct pretend suggestions were coded as successful in two different ways: first, if the child immediately engaged in symbolic play that was both relevant to the suggestion and at or above the level suggested, and second, if suggestions were followed by the toddlers' symbolic play at any level. Indirect support was considered successful if these behaviors were followed by the toddlers' initiation of or continued involvement in symbolic play activity at any level.

Toddler responses to maternal suggestions. The types of behavior that toddlers performed in response to maternal input were coded as either 1) inattention; 2) positive nonpretend responses; or 3) pretend play. Responses coded as "pretend play" were further coded for level of pretend, using a scale based on Fenson's pretend play scale as described in table 3.1.

Reliability

Four "Independent play" and four "Collaborative play" transcripts were randomly selected and coded by two graduate students. Interrater reliability averaged 98 percent on Independent play transcripts and 84 percent on Collaborative play transcripts, with a range of 91 percent to 100 percent and 76 percent to 97 percent, respectively. Remaining tapes were transcribed and coded by one of these graduate students. After coding the first half of the tapes and before coding the second half, one of the earlier transcripts was randomly selected and coded by the graduate student coder to check for consistency in coding across time. Reliability between initial coding and coding at the halfway point was 100 percent for Independent play and 97 percent for Collaborative play tapes.

Results

Dependent T-tests were conducted to compare the frequency, diversity, and complexity of the toddlers' play alone and with mothers. Means and standard deviations for these analyses appear in table 3.2, and the proportions of toddlers engaged in different levels of independence and collaboration with mothers appear in table 3.3.

Dependent T-tests and Pearson correlations were conducted to explore the nature and impact of different types of maternal input into joint symbolic play. Means and standard deviations for repeated measures analyses of variance appear in table 3.4.

Comparisons of Toddlers' Independent and Collaborative Symbolic Play with Mothers

T-tests were conducted to compare the overall frequency, diversity, and level of toddler play in the Independent and Collaborative play sessions. Results of the comparisons between toddler play alone and with mothers appear in tables 3.2 and 3.4.

Toddlers' modal and highest levels of play demonstrated when playing alone, however, were not significantly different from those demonstrated by toddlers playing with their mothers. However, toddlers engaged in signifi-

Table 3.2   Pretend Actions by Level, Alone, and with Mothers

PLAY LEVELS	ALONE		WITH MOTHERS		T	P
	X	SD	X	SD		
Self-directed	1.31	2.31	5.02	5.74	3.62	.001
Passive other	1.52	2.39	8.76	7.19	6.63	.00
Object-directed	1.39	3.59	4.98	4.68	3.92	.00
Active other	.71	2.26	4.48	4.82	4.40	.00
Substitution	.14	.67	1.26	3.13	2.25	.03
Invent 1	.00	.00	2.26	3.98	3.69	.001
Invent 2	.00	.00	.29	.89	2.08	.04
Sequence	1.12	2.04	1.83	2.84	1.40	NS
Multischeme	.88	1.44	4.55	6.90	3.37	.002

Numbers in table represent frequencies of pretend acts.

cantly more overall pretend activity when playing with mothers than when playing alone ($t(41) = 9.38, p < .00$).

Toddlers played at more different levels ($t(38) = 11.16; p < .00$) when playing with mothers than when playing alone. In addition, they exhibited significantly more instances of pretend at eight of nine play levels when playing with mothers than when playing alone ($t(41) = 3.62, p < .001$ for *self-directed pretend;* $t(41) = 6.63, p < .00$ for *passive other-directed pretend;* $t(41) = 3.92, p < .00$ for *object-directed pretend;* $t(41) = 4.40, p < .00$ for *active other-directed pretend;* $t(41) = 2.25, p < .03$ for *substitution;* $t(41) = 3.69, p < .001$ for *invention 1;* $t(41) = 2.08, p < .04$ for *invention 2;* $t(41) = 3.37, p < .02$ for *multischeme combinations*). Further, the proportion of children who demonstrated each play level was greater with mothers than when alone, and increasingly complex play levels appeared at earlier ages when toddlers played with mothers than when they played alone.

Collaborative Symbolic Play

Direct versus indirect input.   Dependent sample T-tests were conducted to compare the frequency of maternal direct and indirect input types, and the success of direct and indirect input types in eliciting toddlers' symbolic play. There was a significant difference between means for both frequency ($t(41) = 3.26, p < .01$) and success ($t(41) = 3.16, p < .01$) of input type.

Mothers made significantly more direct suggestions (m = 39.69) for toddlers' symbolic play than direct input attempts of all forms combined (m = 29.79). Toddlers were also more likely to engage in symbolic play at any level

Table 3.3 Proportion of Toddlers in Each Age Group Engaging in Pretend Levels Alone and with Mothers

							AGE IN MONTHS							
Levels	14–16		17–19		20–22		23–25		26–28		29–33		34–38	
Session*	A	M	A	M	A	M	A	M	A	M	A	M	A	M
Self-directed	.50	.83	.17	.50	.33	1.00	.60	1.00	.33	1.00	.00	.67	.50	1.00
Passive other	.00	1.00	.50	1.00	.33	.83	.40	.83	.33	1.00	.67	1.00	.83	.83
Object-directed	.00	.67	.00	.83	.50	.67	.40	1.00	.33	1.00	.67	1.00	.67	1.00
Active other	.00	.50	.33	.50	.17	.83	.40	.67	.33	.83	.33	1.00	.00	1.00
Single scheme	.17	.67	.17	.33	.17	.67	.60	.50	.67	.83	.67	.50	.83	.33
Multi-scheme	.00	.83	.17	.83	.83	.33	.40	.67	.17	.83	.67	.67	.50	.67
Substitution	.00	.00	.00	.00	.17	.50	.00	.17	.00	.17	.00	.67	.00	.33
Invent 1	.00	.00	.00	.00	.00	.00	.00	.83	.00	.50	.00	.83	.00	.67
Invent 2	.00	.00	.00	.00	.00	.00	.00	.00	.00	.00	.00	.50	.00	.33

* A = alone
M = with Mother

Table 3.4 Frequency and Success of Maternal Input Types

| | TYPE OF INPUT | | | | | |
| | Indirect | | Direct | | *T* | p |
	x	SD	x	SD		
Frequency	29.79	14.08	39.69	16.17	3.26	.01
Success	39%	.19	48%	.19	3.16	.01

Percentages in table represent the percentage of each form of maternal input that was followed by toddlers' performance of pretend activity at any level.

following the mothers' direct suggestion (m = 48 percent of direct suggestions) than following the mothers' indirect input (m = 39 percent of indirect input).

Frequency and Success of Maternal Suggestions

Dependent T-tests were conducted to explore the hypothesis that mothers act as scaffolds for their toddlers' emergent ability to engage in social pretend. T-tests were used to compare the frequency of maternal pretend suggestions made within a range of one level above and below the toddlers' modal play level during the Independent play session with the frequency of maternal suggestions made at all other play levels combined. T-tests also compared the percentage of suggestions made within this modal range that was successfully followed by toddlers' symbolic play at or above the suggested level with the percentage of suggestions made at all other levels combined which was followed by toddler symbolic play.

Mothers were *not* significantly more likely to suggest pretend activities within a range of one level above and below children's modal independent play level than activities at all other levels combined ($t(41) = 1.47$; $p < .15$; within range: m = 17.57; outside range: m = 22.11). Suggestions that were made within the children's modal range, however, were more likely to succeed at engaging toddlers in pretend play at or above the suggested level than suggestions made at all other levels combined ($t(41) = 3.30$; $p < .002$; within range: m = 43%; outside range: m = 30%). Thus, while toddlers were most responsive to suggestions made within the toddlers' modal range of spontaneously exhibited solitary play, mothers did not maximize their potential to influence the toddlers' pretend by consistently suggesting play at these levels. These data imply that adults may have the *potential* to use a zone of proximal development model to guide their input into collaborative symbolic play with toddlers, despite the fact that mothers in the current research did not consistently use this potential.

Frequency and Success of Maternal Indirect Input Types

In addition to making direct suggestions, mothers influenced their toddlers' symbolic play indirectly. Repeated measures analyses of variance were conducted to compare the frequency of different indirect input types, and the percentage of each type that was followed by toddler symbolic play.

Mothers provided *physical assistance* with props and toys (m = 9.62); gave children general *positive support* and feedback for their pretending (m = 8.76); *clarified* children's pretend intentions (m = 4.36); *elaborated* on children's pretend themes, activities, and roles (m = 4.0); *verbalized* about or narrated children's pretend actions (m = 2.48), and *instructed* children in the use of materials (m = 2.07). Mothers were significantly more likely to physically assist their toddlers and provide positive support than to provide other types of indirect input (F (205, 5) = 28.09, $p <$ .000; Scheffe = .01). However, general positive support (m = 47% of all support episodes) and clarification input (m = 39% of all clarification episodes) were significantly more likely to be followed by the toddlers' symbolic play than was instruction (x = 17% of all instruction episodes; F (205, 5) = 6.39, $p <$ .000; Scheffe m = .01 and .05, respectively). Other indirect input forms were equally likely to be followed by toddlers' symbolic play (33 percent of elaboration episodes, 32 percent of assistance episodes, and 23 percent of verbalization episodes).

Frequency and Success of Maternal Input: Relations with Age,
Frequency of Independent Play, and Frequency of
Collaborative Pretend

Pearson correlations were conducted to assess the relation between toddler age, and both the frequency and success of maternal input types in eliciting toddlers' pretend play. Neither the frequency of maternal direct suggestions and toddler age or toddler age and frequency of maternal indirect support were significantly correlated. However, there was a significant correlation between both the percentage of maternal pretend suggestions (r = .65, $p <$ .000) and the percentage of maternal indirect input attempts (r = .57, $p <$ .000) that were followed by pretend response from toddlers and toddler age.

Pearson correlations revealed associations between the mothers' tendency to use particular indirect input types and toddler age. Mothers were less likely to verbalize and narrate their older rather than their younger toddlers' pretend intents and actions (r = -.43, $p <$ .01), but were more likely to elaborate on (r = .38, $p <$ .01) and provide positive support for (r = .38, $p <$ .01) their older than younger toddlers' symbolic play.

Correlations also suggested relations between the mothers' use of particular input forms, and the frequency of the toddlers' independent symbolic play. Toddlers who engaged in more independent symbolic play also received more frequent use of maternal elaboration of their play ($r = .35$, $p < .05$) and instruction ($r = .31$, $p < .05$) during the collaborative play session.

In sum, the frequency of certain input types were associated with age. Similarly, the likelihood that some maternal input forms were followed by the toddlers' symbolic play was also related to the toddlers' age. Older toddlers were more likely than younger toddlers to engage in pretend following maternal physical assistance ($r = .35$, $p < .05$), elaboration ($r = .43$, $p < .01$), and positive support ($r = .33$, $p < .05$).

Finally, both higher frequencies of both maternal direct suggestions ($r = .49$, $p < .001$) and indirect input of all forms combined ($r = .65$, $p < .000$) were associated with higher frequencies of mother-toddler symbolic play. Apparently, more collaborative symbolic play occurred in dyads where mothers offered more input.

Discussion

Toddlers clearly engaged in more elaborate symbolic pretend play with their mothers than when playing alone in the current study. As several investigators (Schaffer 1984) have noted, however, the relative contributions of adults and young children to joint activities must be assessed prior to concluding that toddlers are competent at performing complex tasks. Vygotsky has suggested (1962, 1978) that adults may help children to accomplish what they cannot accomplish on their own—that is, to operate within their zone of proximal, rather than actual, development. Adults may be largely responsible for the apparently smooth flow of difficult activities performed by adults and children, at least until the children are capable of carrying out these activities independently.

It is difficult to determine from the current study whether mothers were generally responsible for structuring children's pretend activity, or whether children initiated activities that mothers then joined or followed. The findings that mothers did frequently suggest and encourage toddlers to pretend, and that the toddlers' pretend was more frequent, varied, and elaborate with mothers than when alone, tentatively suggests that mothers might be responsible for the complexity and frequency of pretend in the mother-toddler condition. Greater frequencies of collaborative symbolic play were associated with greater frequencies of maternal suggestions and indirect input. However, higher frequencies of at least some forms of maternal input were also associated with higher frequencies of the toddlers' independent symbolic play. These findings raise important questions regarding the direction of effects. That is, does more play occur because maternal input facilitates the toddlers' symbolic play in the collaborative setting, or children who happen to be avid and skilled pretenders elicit more interaction from mothers? In sum, whether mothers in this study were influencing or responding to their children's play capacities is not entirely clear.

Perhaps maternal input is largely responsible for the increased symbolic play in the collaborative condition. Especially with young toddlers, mothers may be more likely to initiate pretend, and better able to interpret the toddlers' pretend overtures and maintain social interaction than are same-aged toddler peers. As Howes (Howes 1985; Howes, Unger, & Seidner 1989) has suggested, toddlers may be able to pretend play before they can talk about, plan, or carry on pretend smoothly with a partner. Competent adults may assist toddlers in pretending by assuming responsibility for talking about, planning, and maintaining the pretend structure within which toddlers are capable of pretending before toddlers are able to manage these responsibilities on their own. Alternately, as toddlers grow older, they may become more skilled managers of pretend interactions. The findings that mothers are more likely to verbalize about the pretend of younger toddlers, and to elaborate on or merely provide positive support for older players suggests that the mother's role in pretend may shift from that of play manager to partner and audience as children gradually assume a more managerial role.

The issue of direction of effects returns this chapter to the question of maternal input models raised in the introduction. Do mothers operate within a zone of proximal development model, a smorgasbord model, or a scaffolding model of adult input into toddler symbolic play? Perhaps the best answer that the current study can provide is "yes and no."

The hypothesis that mothers function within a zone of proximal development model received only partial support from the data. As this model would predict, maternal suggestions made within a range around the children's modal, unassisted play level were more successful at engaging children in pretend than were suggestions made at all other levels combined. However, mothers made fewer suggestions within this modal range than at all other levels combined.

At first glance, these findings lend support to O'Connell and Bretherton's (1984) claim that mothers may offer children a smorgasbord of suggestions from which children select those which approximate their ability and understanding, rather than providing suggestions that approximate children's capacities. Alternatively, the finding that mothers did not make the majority of their pretend suggestions within their children's modal play ranges may be due more to methodological factors than to the mother's lack of sensitivity or child development knowledge. Comparing mothers' input to extant play scales may be a deceptive way to judge whether mothers act within the zone of proximal development for their toddlers' play.

It is not entirely surprising that, when playing with their toddlers, mothers do not follow a symbolic play scale derived from and for academic research. However, it is possible that mothers unconsciously or consciously structure their suggestions for their toddlers' symbolic play according to another system which is, as yet, unavailable to the researcher. For example, during observations of mothers and toddlers, the mothers seemed to organize their input into their toddlers' play more thematically than in terms of increasing decentration and integration, which is the underlying organization of the Fenson symbolic play scale. In order to learn more about the mothers' own systems of organizing children's play, future research should explore the organization that mothers may impose on their play with toddlers, rather than imposing a particular research tool on maternal input.

Finally, results provide some evidence that adults serve as scaffolds to support their toddlers' emerging symbolic play capacities. As DeLoache and Plaetzer explain:

> The suggestions, demonstrations, corrections, and elaborations that predominate in the mother's behavior represent clear forms of scaffolding: they provide structure for interaction and support for the child's efforts. (DeLoache & Plaetzer 1985, 10–11)

Mothers in this study made younger toddlers' first, and sometimes shaky, attempts at pretend explicit; physically assisted older toddlers who were more capable of pretend but still a bit uncoordinated and needeing some help arranging props; and encouraged elaborate pretend by still more competent players. Mothers seemed to be equally likely to suggest pretend activities to older and younger children, but became less directive and more likely to observe and support the toddlers' independent play ideas as the toddlers grew older, and became more competent pretenders. In short, mothers appeared to handle those elements of pretend that toddlers could not manage, and to relinquish the control of pretend to the toddlers as their capacities increased.

Results reinforce the complexity of relationships between maternal and toddler input in the construction of early social pretend. Both mothers and toddlers play a role in weaving pretend themes, but precisely how these roles develop and affect one another is still unclear, and deserves attention in future research.

4

Collaborative Construction of Social Pretend Play between Toddler-Age Partners: Illustrative Study #2

Carollee Howes and Olivia Unger

By two years of age children are beginning to engage in social pretend play (Dunn & Dale 1984; Howes 1985). The development of social pretend play parallels advances in the communication of meaning between peers (Howes 1987) and more general advances in linguistic and cognitive development (Brownell 1986). While toddler social pretend play has been described, the extant literature has only begun to examine the manner in which these young children construct social pretend play. The purpose of the current study was to describe and compare the efficacy of strategies used by toddlers to construct social pretend play with their peers.

Previous research on the joint construction of social pretend play has focused on mother-toddler social pretend play (Adler & McCune 1985; Dunn & Dale 1984; O'Connell & Bretherton 1984) and preschool peer social pretend play (Garvey 1977; Nelson & Seidman 1984). While each of these contexts for social pretend play differs from the toddler-peer context, this literature can serve as a guide to understanding the construction of toddler social pretend play. Mother-child social pretend play differs from toddler social pretend play in that one actor has more knowledge of how to play the game than the other. Studies of mother-child game playing suggest that mothers provide a framework or social "scaffold" for the child's acquisition of skills (Bruner 1978). Maternal behaviors serve to direct the child's attention to the play and to set the stage for the child's reciprocal or turn-taking action (Hodapp, Goldfield, & Boyatzis 1984). Within joint mother-child play, mothers tend to make obligatory moves (Adler & McCune 1985). Obligatory moves are behaviors such as direct or request information that require or strongly expect a response from the partner. These moves or behaviors are instrumental in maintaining the joint play.

The study of toddler social pretend play presents an opportunity to examine strategies used by toddlers that serve the same function as strategies used by experienced players such as mothers. Therefore, in the current study it was hypothesized that toddler social strategies that were obligatory or by their content required a response from the partner would be more effective than those which required no response from the partner. For example, it was assumed that simply watching the pretend action of the partner does not require a response from the partner and is, therefore, unlikely to elicit joint play, while commanding the partner to engage in a pretend act because it requires a response is more likely to direct the partner's attention to joint activity.

Furthermore, several researchers of mother-child play report that mothers provide children with suggestions for and demonstrations of play activities (O'Connell & Bretherton 1984; Schaffer & Crook 1979). The most effective maternal strategies for modifying the child's play activities appear to be the strategies that match or coincide with the interests of the child (O'Connell & Bretherton 1984; Schaffer 1984). Thus, in the current study, strategies that were dependent on the pretend action of the partner were expected to be more effective in producing social pretend play than strategies independent of the pretend action of the partner. There was also expected to be an interaction between the obligatory nature of the strategy and the strategy's independence of the pretend act of the partner. Strategies that required a response from the partner and that were dependent on the pretend act of the partner were expected to be most effective in producing social pretend play. Such strategies were assumed to be most effective in eliciting joint play because the child has accommodated to the other child and provided a mechanism for her response.

Method

Subject

Forty-two children (twenty-two girls) participated in this study. Six children were selected from each of the three month age intervals between fourteen and twenty-eight months and six children were selected from each of the two five-month age intervals between twenty-nine and thirty-eight months. Age intervals were smaller prior to twenty-nine months because changes in play as well as the pace of development in general were expected to be most dramatic at earlier ages. Each child was paired with another according to the following criteria: the children were within six weeks of the same age, both children fell into the same age interval, and the children had played together at least weekly for at least three months. All of the children were from well-educated families in an urban geographic area. Sixty percent of the children were Anglo in ethnic background, the remainder were Black or Asian. The children were recruited through parent education and gym classes, and child-care centers.

For the purposes of the current analysis, children were grouped into the following age categories: fourteen to twenty-two months (n = 18); twenty-three to twenty-nine months (n = 12); and twenty-nine to thirty-eight months (n = 12). These age groupings were selected because previous research suggests that changes in social pretend play forms occur at about twenty-four and thirty months (Howes, Unger, & Seidner 1989).

Procedures

Children were observed and videotaped during a fifteen-minute play session. Children played with a standard set of toys selected to maximize the likelihood of both pretend play and social interaction. Each toy was provided in duplicate so that each child could play with the same toy. The selected toys were: blocks, snap-together plastic toys, a small table and two chairs, cups, plates, spoons, pitchers, baby bottles, hair brushes, combs, mirrors, cars, small action figures, dolls, telephones, cradles, blankets, high chairs, and strollers.

The livingroom or playroom of the randomly selected home was cleared of other toys and the experimental toys were arranged in a standard order on the floor. The mothers were asked to remain to the side or in an adjoining room and to let the children play without interference.

Measures

The children's play with peers was coded for both social play forms (coded as dyadic measures) and for social strategies (coded as individual measures).

Social pretend play. Social pretend play was defined as the integration of pretense into social interaction between partners. In order to be considered social pretend play the social interaction had at least a turn-taking structure. Three forms of social pretend play were considered in the current analyses.

Simple social pretend play was coded if the children engaged in social play and both children performed pretend acts. The acts may have been temporally related or have involved similar toys but there was no script. A script was defined as an organized, multievent play sequence in which the two children arrange pretend acts into a meaningful sequence (Nelson & Seidman 1984).

Associate social pretend play was coded if the children engaged in social play, there was a script but no complementary pretend roles. Complementary pretend roles were defined as roles that are in relation to the other (e.g., mother–baby, fire-fighter–person in a burning building).

Cooperative was coded if the children engaged in social play, there was a script and complementary pretend roles. Roles did not have to be explicitly named but the role must have been clear from the action (e.g., A feeds B with bottle, B drinks and cries like a baby).

Previous research with these social pretend play forms suggests that they represent increased complexity in social pretend play from simple social to cooperative (Howes 1985; Howes & Farver 1987; Howes, Unger, & Seidner 1989).

Social strategies.   Nineteen different social behaviors were identified from the videotapes as strategies used by the children to construct social pretend play. These strategies and their definitions are presented in table 4.1.

Coding and Reliability

As the primary focus of the current study was on competence rather than performance, behaviors were coded as present or absent. This approach avoided some of the problems of low-frequency data which is endemic to research on young children's play (see Fein, Moorin, & Enslein 1982; McCune-Nicolich 1981).

The sequence of strategies and social play forms was transcribed from the videotapes into transcript form. Intercoder reliability for preparing transcripts was initially established to a 95 percent criterion (agreements/agreements + disagreements + omissions) on all codes on five randomly selected videotapes. Intercoder reliability was re-established to the same criterion on four randomly selected videotapes both at midpoint and at the end of coding.

The transcripts were then coded for the presence or absence of both strategies and social pretend play. For the effectiveness of strategies in the construction of social pretend play, a strategy was considered effective if social play followed the strategy. Intercoder reliability for these measures was established and maintained to 95 percent criterion as described above.

Table 4.1 Social Strategies, Their Definitions, and Classifications

		CLASSIFICATION	
Social behavior	Definition	Pretend Response (R/NR)	action (I/D)
Watch	eye gaze at pretend action of the partner (34)	NR	D
Imitation immediate	imitation of pretend action of partner within 10 seconds (15)	NR	D
delayed	imitation of pretend action of partner after delay of 1 minute or more (8)	NR	D
Recruit nonverbal	children are not engaged in social pretend play; child performs a pretend act and directs it to the partner by eye gaze, gesture, or by offering toy (17)	R	I
verbal	children are not engaged in social pretend play; child performed a pretend act and named it to the partner (8)	R	I
Join	following the partner's solitary pretend act; child directs a pretend act to the partner or names the pretend act as described in recruit strategy (5)	R	D
Comment other	the child verbally labels the pretend act of the partner (9)	R	D
own	the child verbally labels her own pretend act without eye contact with the partner (17)	NR	I
Command verbal	the child directs the partner to perform a specific pretend act (8)	R	I
nonverbal	the child points, hands the partner a toy, or demonstrates an action while maintaining eye contact with the partner (11)	R	I

Table 4.1   *Continued*

		CLASSIFICATION	
Social behavior	Definition	Pretend Response (R/NR)	action (I/D)
Return	the partner engaged in a pretend act, the toy used in pretend falls or is knocked over, and the child retrieves the toy for the partner (6)	R	D
Set stage	the child moves and organizes toys to facilitate pretend acts on a combination of toys (22)	NR	I
Set stage partner	the child moves and organizes two sets of toys to facilitate pretend acts on a combination of toys (11)	R	I
Search	the child searches for a complementary toy to a pretend act just performed; the child has to label and/or find the object (10)	NR	I
Negotiate	the child and the partner verbally discuss the theme of the pretend play (4)	R	D

Note: Number in parentheses indicates number of children engaging in behavior;
I = independent, D = dependent, R = required, N = not required = nonclassifiable.

Classification of strategies.   Each category was conceptually classified on two dimensions. The dimensions were: Requires a response from the
partner versus no response; and dependent on the pretend action of the partner versus independent. The classification of each strategy is also presented
in table 4.1.

Data Analysis

The plan of data analysis was first to examine age differences in the
use and effectiveness of strategies with different classifications and to compare the effectiveness of strategies of different classifications. The number of
children to use each category of strategy and the number of children for

whom the strategy was effective in producing social pretend play were calculated and compared. All comparisons were made with chi squares. Only those comparisons with chi square values with probabilities values of less than .05 are reported in the text.

Comparison of Strategies that Did and Did Not Require A Response From the Partner

In order to examine the hypothesis that strategies requiring a response from the partner would be more effective in eliciting joint pretend play strategies than strategies that did not require a response, these two strategy types were compared. The percentage of children using each type of strategy and the percentage for whom the strategies were effective in producing social pretend play are presented in table 4.2.

Age differences.   As the age of the children increased, so did the use of both types of strategies (required a response: $\chi^2(2) = 14.27$, $p = .008$; no response required: $\chi^2(2) = 17.50$, $p = .002$). Similar numbers of children used each type of strategy in each age group. Both types of strategies were more likely to result in social pretend play in the older age groups than in the youngest (required a response: $\chi^2(2) = 13.42$, $p = .001$; no response required: $\chi^2(2) = 26.19$, $p = .001$).

Differences in effectiveness.   Strategies that required a response were equally successful in eliciting any social pretend play, simple social pretend play, and associative social pretend play, as were strategies that did not require a response. However, strategies that required a response more often elicited cooperative social pretend play while strategies that did not require a response more often elicited simple social pretend play ($\chi^2(1) = 14.32$, $p = .001$). Therefore, the hypothesis that strategies that required a response would be more effective in eliciting social pretend play was partially supported.

Comparison of Strategies That Are and Are Not Dependent on the Play Action of the Partner

In order to examine the hypothesis that strategies dependent on the pretend act of the partner would be more effective in eliciting joint pretend play than strategies independent of the partner's action, independent and dependent strategies were compared. The percentage of children to use both types of strategies and the percentage for whom the strategies were effective in producing social pretend play are also presented in table 4.2.

Table 4.2   Comparison of Strategies that Require a Response from the Partner and are Dependent on Pretend Action of the Partner

		PERCENT OF GROUP SUCCESSFULLY USED STRATEGY TO ACHIEVE			
	Percentage of group used strategy	any play	simple play	associative play	cooperative play
		Response required			
Dependent on the pretend act of the partner					
Age in months					
14 to 22	6	0	0	0	0
23 to 28	42	67	0	17	50
29 to 38	83	83	42	0	75
Independent of the pretend act of the partner					
Age in months					
14 to 22	44	0	0	0	0
23 to 28	92	42	8	17	17
29 to 38	100	50	8	0	42
		No response required			
Dependent on the pretend act of the partner					
Age in months					
14 to 22	67	11	11	0	0
23 to 28	92	42	24	17	0
29 to 38	100	58	33	25	0
Independent of the pretend act of the partner					
Age in months					
14 to 22	6	0	0	0	0
23 to 28	92	17	17	0	0
29 to 38	100	42	25	17	0

Note: Numbers tabled reflect percent of group.

Age differences.   As age increased so did the use of both strategies dependent on and independent of the partner's action (dependent: $\chi^2(2) = 17.50$, $p = .002$; independent: $\chi^2(2) = 11.20$, $p = .004$). Similar numbers of children used each type of strategy in each age group. Both strategy types were more effective in eliciting social pretend play in the older age groups than in the youngest (dependent: $\chi^2(2) = 22.04$, $p = .004$; independent: $\chi^2(2) = 21.51$, $p = .001$).

Differences in effectiveness. Dependent and independent strategies were equally effective in eliciting any and all forms of social pretend play. Therefore, the hypothesis that strategies dependent on the pretend action of the partner would be more effective than strategies independent of the pretend action of the partner was not supported.

Strategies That Require a Response and Are Dependent on the Pretend Act of the Partner

Finally, the interaction between requiring a response and dependence on the pretend actions of the partners was examined. Strategies that were both dependent on the pretend action of the partner and required a response were expected to be most effective in eliciting social pretend play. In making these comparisons, the number of children who used and used effectively strategies that were dependent on the pretend act of the partner *and* required a response were compared to the number of children who used and used effectively the other types of strategies (independent of the partner and requiring a response, dependent of the partner and not requiring a response, or independent or the partner and not requiring a response).

Age differences. The number of children who used strategies both dependent on the pretend action of the partner *and* requiring a response increased between each age group ($\chi^2(2) = 11.4$, $p = .003$; Fisher exact tests $= .05$) while the number of children who used the other strategy types increased only between the first and second age groups ($\chi^2(2) = 9.73$, $p = .007$; Fisher exact tests $=$ ns). Fewer children in each age group used strategies both dependent on the pretend action of the partner *and* requiring a response than used other strategies ($\chi^2(2) = 6.60$, $p = .04$). Both types of strategies were more effective in eliciting social pretend play in the older age groups than in the youngest (dependent *and* requiring a response: ($\chi^2(2) = 9.73$, $p = .01$; other: ($\chi^2(2) = 9.63$, $p = .01$).

Differences in effectiveness. Strategies that were dependent on the pretend action of the partner and required a response were more effective in eliciting social pretend play ($\chi^2(1) = 6.86$, $p = .02$) and in eliciting cooperative social pretend play ($\chi^2(1) = 11.48$, $p = .001$) than the other strategies. There were no differences in the effectiveness of the two types of strategies in eliciting less complex forms of social pretend play. Therefore, the hypotheses that strategies that were dependent on the pretend action of the partner and required a response would be most effective in eliciting social pretend play were supported.

Discussion

The current research suggests that in lieu of an experienced and knowledgeable social partner toddlers use strategies to elicit social pretend play that are functionally similar to those used by adults and older peers when they play social pretend with the child. By twenty-nine to thirty-eight months of age almost all of the toddlers in the current study used strategies that accommodated to the partner by requiring a response and by being dependent on the pretend action of the partner. Thus, as has been demonstrated with social play and language (Mueller et al. 1977), within the context of joint play two-year-old peers are able to adjust their communicative behaviors to the perceived needs of the partner.

Accommodating the partner by requiring a response and linking the strategy to her pretend action appear similar to the social-cognitive skills suggested by Rose-Krasnor (1983) as essential to successful social problem solving. If the child accommodates her strategies to the partner's behavior, it appears as if the child has a social goal that of constructing social pretend play, and some beginning ability to perceive and process social information, to anticipate and understand social behaviors of the other and to anticipate and understand social outcomes. Connolly and Doyle (1984) have suggested that social pretend play may mediate between social interaction skills with peers and social competency. The results of the current study suggest one mechanism for this relationship. The construction of social pretend play between toddlers may provide a context for acquiring some of the social cognitions inherent in social competence.

5

An Analysis of Young American and Mexican Children's Play Dialogues[2]: Illustrative Study #3

JoAnn M. Farver

In the past, numerous ethnographies have documented that young children in many societies of the world engage in some form of symbolic play behavior (Raum 1940; Bascom 1969; Centner 1962; Storey 1976; Lancy 1977). However, it is not clear from these accounts how children in other than Western cultures begin to understand, share, and integrate each other's imaginative constructions.

Abundant research with American children has shown that by age three, children engage in coherent discourse (Keenan 1974; Mueller 1972), play collaboratively (Garvey & Berndt 1977), superimpose story lines on their play dialogues (Garvey & Berndt 1977; Schwartzman 1976; Forys & McCune-Nicolich 1984), and enact roles (Garvey & Berndt 1977; Sachs 1980; Forys & McCune-Nicolich 1984; Rubin 1980). Jointly constructed pretend play episodes require considerable conceptual, communicative, and social skills from young participants (Fein & Schwartz 1986; Howes 1985; Brenner & Mueller 1982). Developmental theorists postulate that young children begin to coordinate their imaginative constructions with a partner by linking their expanding social knowledge with features of the interactive play experience through conversation (Seidman 1983; Sachs, Goldman & Chaille 1984, 1985; Goncu & Kessel 1984; Corsaro & Tomlinson 1979; Corsaro 1983; 1986).

For example, according to Bateson (1971) play can only occur if participants are able to exchange metacommunicative signals that convey the message "This is play." Therefore, to initiate and sustain social pretend play, partners must keep each other informed about the change from nonplay to play while continuing to make their play actions mutually intelligible.

In a number of studies, Garvey (1974; 1977; 1984; Garvey & Berndt 1977) has noted that much of children's talk is directed to creating, clarifying, maintaining, and negotiating the social pretend experience. During the course of play children must pay attention to the partner's actions and verbalizations and consistently acknowledge and make contributions accordingly.

Corsaro's extensive analyses of children's play dialogues indicate that children rely on particular communicative strategies during interactive play to make their actions and ideas intelligible and thus potentially shareable with a partner (Corsaro & Tomlinson 1979; Corsaro 1986; Cook-Gumperez & Corsaro 1977). Further research in this area has shown that there is a developmental progression in children's use of the conversational strategies identified by Corsaro. Children begin to use strategies when they are as young as two years of age and become quite skilled by the age of five (Farver 1989).

Although there has been no published work on the play of Mexican children, preliminary results from a recent study of Mexican children's social behavior indicate that their play follows a developmental pattern similar to that of American children, and that they engage in lively discourse during play activity (Farver 1989).

The purpose of this study is to investigate how young children use communicative strategies to structure and create shared meaning in pretend play by examining the play dialogues of American and Mexican three-year-old children. This analysis serves as a step in assessing the generalizability of earlier findings regarding basic features of children's use of communicative strategies.

Method

Subjects

Subjects of this research were thirty-two (n = 16 girls) three-year-old children (M = 38 months). The sixteen Mexican children lived in extended family households in a working-class village located on the Pacific Coast. Residents of the community were very sociable. Commonly, women sat together during the day sewing, watching TV novellas, or talking while their children played outdoors together. Three-year-olds rarely wandered far from their homes without the company of an older sibling. There were few manufactured toys in the homes, but the children were highly imaginative with household objects and improvised toys.

The sixteen American children lived in single-family homes in Northern California. The children were homogeneous with regard to ethnicity and came from working-class families. Few mothers worked outside the home and their children had little or no day-care experience. Three-year-olds generally spent their days in the company of their mothers or older siblings and occasionally in informal play groups organized by neighbors.

Procedures

Children in both cultures were videotaped in their homes while playing with a bag of wooden shapes with a same-sex and age partner for twenty minutes. The wooden shapes included humanlike figures, arches, block shapes (suggestive of houses, bridges, churches), farm animals, tree figures, and train pieces. The shapes provided suggestions for pretense without introducing "toys" from either culture, and rendered play behaviors in the two cultures comparable. The shapes were spread out on a convenient table and the children were asked to play with them. The observer sat quietly nearby recording relevant contextual information.

Coding of Play Dialogues

Videotapes were fully transcribed. Transcriptions were segmented into interactive play episodes. An episode was defined as an interactive sequence occurring between two children containing three or more exchanges of continuous discourse with a shared theme or topic. An episode began when one child verbalized about an object, action, activity, or feeling state, and terminated when the partner failed to address the topic of the preceding turn, talk was interrupted by environmental interference, or either child physically moved away from the play activity.

The unit of analysis was the interactive turn (defined as all of one partner's utterances before the other partner took the floor). Transcribed play dialogues were coded by episode. Each play episode was examined by conversational turn for duration (number of exchanges), seven communicative strategies, structure of the interaction, and thematic content.

Measures

The data base for this analysis consisted of ninety transcribed episodes randomly selected from each culture, (USA N = 45; Mexico N = 45).

Communicative Strategies

Seven communicative strategies identified by Corsaro (1986) were considered. Strategies were scored for the number of times each occurred during an episode.

(1) *Paralinguistic cues:* Changes in intonation and pitch to mark fantasy and the animation of objects. For example, the "vrroom vrroom" sounds of toy car engines; "nyam nyam" sound of pretend eating, and the use of high or low voices to mark role enactment.

(2) *Descriptions of action:* Declarative statements that accompany ongoing activity or describe past or future action. For example, Child A. says, "I'm going into the forest," as she moves the toy jeep to the corner of the table.

(3) *Repetitions:* Repeating of prior utterance(s) of the partner.

(4) *Semantic tying:* Additions of new semantic elements to the partner's previous contribution. For example: Child A: "It's raining. Gonna rain." Child B: "Rain! It's gonna be a rainstorm."

(5) *Calls for attention:* Utterances used to gain the partner's attention or request aid and include: partner's name, "Hey!," "Look!," or "Help!," etc.

(6) *Directive:* Declaratives used to control the partner's action. For example: "DO this!"; "YOU put the man on the train!"; "No, DON'T go in there!"

(7) *Tags:* Verbal devices normally placed at the end of a conversational turn and are used to elicit a response or acknowledgment. These include: "This is a blue man, isn't it?"; "We're gonna have lunch with Santa Claus, right?"

Structure of the Interaction

Children's social behaviors in play described by Garvey (1984) were condensed into four categories. Social behaviors were scored for the number of times they occurred during the episode.

(1) *Initiate play:* Child attracts partner's attention by speaking while examining objects in the environment, by verbalizing an action, or

by explicitly inviting the partner to play. For example, "Look what I'm making," or "I'm makin' coffee," or "Do you want to play camping?"

(2) *Establish common reference:* Children allocate materials' name objects, invent objects or roles. For example, "It's a man," "It's dinner time," "You be the mommy and I'll be the daddy."

(3) *Coordinate action:* Children construct a joint line of action and discourse where each child builds on the partner's turn. The content or meaning gives the episode its cohesion. For example, A: "Pretend that this is a swimming pool and we have to go take our swimming lessons." B: "And mommy isn't going to watch us, ok? Because she has to get frosties."

(4) *Enactment:* Partners enact a shared script. No transformations are proposed. All meanings have been previously established by preceding discussion or by tradition.

Thematic Content

Exchanges that evoke or sustain a fantasy or imaginative context were coded using a scale developed by Rosenberg (1985).

(1) *Positive:* This category includes family relations, caretaking, and nurturance. For example, the child sets up a family structure or identifies characters as family members and displays positive actions such as nurturance, cooking food, or caring for a brother or sister.

(2) *Negative:* This category includes aggression and danger in the environment. It is characterized by crashing, running over with vehicles, murder, or throwing toys. Danger is reflected in themes concerning chaos, disasters, accidents, storms, illnesses, or injuries.

(3) *Conflict:* This category includes conflicted relations, authority, and control issues. For example, two persons are represented in a fantasy who are in conflict, or the subject (while in fantasy play) assumes a role of a character in a struggle or conflict. Tone of voice, verbal content, and behaviors are all signs of conflicted relations.

(4) *Affiliation:* This category includes fantasy activities that are adult-like in social behavior. For example, going to a cocktail party, or driving on the freeway to a campground.

Intercoder Reliability

Reliability was established between the author and a bilingual, bicultural assistant using twenty (ten from each culture), randomly chosen interactive play episodes that were not part of the data base for the present study. Cohen's Kappa values for agreement on coding the duration of the episodes, scoring of the communicative strategies, children's social behaviors in play, and thematic content ranged from .83 to .96.

Results and Discussion

Communicative Strategies

Children in both cultures used communicative strategies to structure their play episodes. Frequencies of these strategies are in table 5.1. The most common strategy was to describe actions. This strategy may have been particularly tied to the properties of the task. When presented with wooden shapes the children provided descriptive labels linked to their physical properties (i.e., color, size, and literal representation). The following dialogue created by a Mexican dyad illustrates describing actions:

> A: Look at these pines here (A picks up a tree shape and shows it to B.) And another over here. There are many pines. Look for all the pines.
>
> B: Another!

The next most frequent strategy was paralinguistic cues. Paralinguistic cues signaled to partners that a play object had become something other than

Table 5.1   Communicative Strategies

STRATEGIES	NUMBER OF INSTANCES
Describe action	221
Paralinguistic cues	154
Directive	125
Call for attention	62
Repetition	50
Tag	30
Semantic tie	20

it appeared. For example, a block moving through the air became an airplane when accompanied by a "vrroom vrroom" sound. Paralinguistic cues were used often in play dialogues because they require minimal cognitive processing from young players and, therefore, make it easier for partners to share and contribute to the pretense. Most common to each culture was the "vroom vroom" sound given to engines.

Directives were used to elaborate play. The dialogue between the Mexican children continues:

A: Good, the tree goes up here.

B: Here?

A: No! Put the tree up here.

The other, more complex strategies were used less frequently. Nevertheless, when used they served to continue themes and add new dimensions to the story lines. The following sequence from an American dyad shows how Child B's semantic ties build on Child A's play suggestions:

A: Pretend it was Christmas Time, OK?

B: (nods agreement)

A: And he said, "Santa's comin'."

B: And this guy was Santa (picking up human figure).

A: And he said, "Hurrah! Santa's comin'."

B: And the train was comin' and the Santa was in the train. Choo Choo Choo Choo...Choo (B puts figure on train and moves train toward A).

Structure of Play Interaction

The children used all four types of structuring of the play interaction. See table 5.2. The most frequent form of structuring was through establishing a common reference.

In the example below, two American partners establish common reference by naming objects and telling each other what they are doing with them. In the process a simple story begins to unfold:

A: And here's a table where we could eat our lunch on (A picks up block shape).

Table 5.2   Structuring of Play Interaction

STRUCTURING STRATEGIES	NUMBER OF INSTANCES
Establish a common reference	228
Coordinate action	221
Initiate play	94
Enactment	34

B: But first we gotta get the chairs. Here's a chair (B picks up rectangular pieces and puts them near A's block "table"). Here's one for Santa and here's one for the children. And I said, "Santa's dinner's ready!"

A: Oh yummy yummy!

B: But first, you have to wait for the dog. (B sets a dog shape near the "table.")

A: Oh, Santa dog is here!

B: No, you knocked over our lunch. (Pieces fall over.)

A: Woof! Woof!

The second most frequent form of structuring was to coordinate actions. This structure also led to the creation of a story line as in the following episode about bricklaying created by a Mexican dyad.

A: Give me the bricks. (Takes rectangular shapes from B and begins a stack.) Look at the bricks. Hurry up! A man is going to make bricks. Bring me the bricks.

B: Look, here is another brick (hands another rectangular shape to A).

The two other forms of structuring, initiating play and enactment, appeared less frequently in the children's play and appeared less likely to lead the children into a social pretend play episode.

Conversational contributions were tied to the physical properties of the shapes (i.e., color, size, and literal representation). Mexican children labeled the play shapes and coordinated actions with them. They used calls for attention to initiate and display their involvement in play. Elaborative suggestions for play were offered by means of directives.

Thematic Content

Almost half (49 percent) of the episodes were positive in theme and 29 percent were affiliative. Only 13 percent of the episodes were aggressive and 9 percent conflictual. Thematic content of the play episodes mirrored activities that were familiar to the children and characteristic of the individual culture. Since the American data collection occurred around Christmastime, children incorporated holiday themes in their play. For example, children fantasized "going to the mountains to cut down a Christmas tree" (a common December activity in Northern California) and "having lunch with Santa Claus."

Mexican children drove "trucks" (the train shapes) to the neighboring big city, gave rides to "Nacho" (a popular cartoon mouse in Mexican comics and TV), built houses out of "bricks" (rectangular shapes), and made "ranchitos" (small ranches) with farm animals.

With regard to the overall characteristics of the play episodes it is interesting to note that children in neither culture offered a specific plan of action or negotiated their play. Play sequences were made up of spontaneous comments about the shapes themselves, or the partner's actions and verbalizations. In this sense, play in both cultures had a dynamic quality. Children seemed to construct shared meaning during the course of their play by building on their partner's ideas and actions as the play unfolded. This finding concurs with Goncu and Kessel's (1984) research that noted that the play of young children is unmarked by explicit verbal negotiation. This conclusion is also consistent with studies reviewed by Fein and Schwartz (1986, 53) who claim that play sequences do not have scripts per se, but are constructed "bottom up" by the players as the exchanges progress. Because the sequences are invented by the players spontaneously, not even the children know what will happen next.

Part II

NEGOTIATING SOCIAL PRETEND PLAY:
ISSUES OF CONTROL AND COMPROMISE

6

*Expressing and Exploring Issues of Control and
Compromise by Negotiating Social Pretend Play
Meanings and Scripts*

Within our framework the function of social pretend play during the early preschool years is to explore issues of control and compromise. Issues of control and compromise are expressed by negotiations within social pretend play. By thirty to thirty-six months of age most children who have had experience with peers or siblings are able to engage in social pretend play with age-mates (Dunn & Dale 1984; Forys & McCune-Nicolich 1984; Garvey 1982; Garvey & Berndt 1977; Goncu 1987; Howes 1985; 1988; Howes & Unger 1989; Howes et al. 1989; Iwanaga 1973). However, social pretend play between peers is still not smooth and easily flowing. Partners spend endless amounts of time assigning and negotiating play roles ("I want to be the mother," "You are always the mother, I'm the mother this time"), scripts ("Now you are dead, I shot you," "No, I'm not really dead, I got well and I'm going to steal the money") and themes ("Pretend we go to the zoo," "And when we are at the zoo I have to go right to the hospital because I'm sick") of the play. While several researchers (e.g., Garvey 1977; Griffin 1984) have described these negotiations as illustrative of the development of metacommunication skills, the negotiations also function as a means for children to explore issues of control and compromise. Autonomy, control, and compromise with others are important issues for two- and three-year-old children (Erikson 1950; 1964; Kopp 1982). We suggest that these issues are explored within social pretend play as well as in other more traditional arenas (compliance with adults and toilet training).

Our literature search for descriptive studies of social pretend play between thirty-seven and forty-eight months yielded twenty-two different studies. These are presented in table 6.1. The negotiations which first emerged in studies of children between thirty-one and thirty-six months are a predominant feature of play during the thirty-seven to forty-eight-month period. All of the studies of social pretend play with children over three studied only play between peer partners. Adults and older siblings were no longer included.

Changing Functions and Partners for Social Pretend Play

We suspect that the changing function of social pretend play is related to changing partners. Bryant (1989) suggests that within each stage of development the need to master autonomy is balanced by the need to master

Table 6.1 Expressing and Exploring Issues of Control and Compromise by Negotiating Social Pretend Play Meanings and Scripts

| | PARTNER | |
Adult	Older Sib	Peer
31–36 months		
Mother praises and encourages independence. May engage in joint pretend.[a]	Joint development of play and joint role play.[b]	Joint pretend with enactment of complementary roles. Children discriminate between speech used for enactment and speech used for enactment and speech about enactment. Children assign roles and negotiate pretend themes and plans.[c]
37–48 months		
		Children adopt relational roles, are willing to accept identity transformations and generate or accept instruction for appropriate role performance. Children negotiate scripts and dominant roles and use metacommunication to establish the play script and clarify role enactment.[d]

Table 6.1   *(continued)*

Adult	PARTNER Older Sib	Peer

49–65 months

		Play has an integrative structure of differential roles. The roles are discussed and assigned, enacted interactively, and the role behavior of each partner continuously influences the other. New information is added to play scripts during pretend.[e]

[a] Farver 1989; Fiese 1988.

[b] Farver 1989.

[c] Forys & McCune-Nicolich 1984; Garvey 1982; Garvey & Berndt 1977; Goncu 1987; Howes 1985; Howes & Unger 1987; Howes et al. 1989; Iwanaga 1973.

[d] Field, DeStefano, & Koewler 1982; Garvey 1982; Garvey & Berndt 1977; Giffin 1984; Goncu & Kessel 1984; Iwanaga 1973; McLoyd 1980; 1985; McLoyd, Thomas, & Warren 1984; Sachs et al. 1984; Saunders & Harper 1976.

[e] Doyle & Connolly 1989; Connolly, Doyle & Reznick 1988; Field et al. 1982; Genishi 1983; Goncu 1987; Iwanaga 1973; Mathews 1977; Nelson & Seidman 1984; Pellegrini 1985; Sachs et al. 1984.

connections to others. Social pretend play with the mother once children have mastered the pretend play forms illustrates this balance. Mothers may best support the development of social pretend play in older children by providing opportunities for and approval of social pretence but avoiding being drawn into negotiations over themes, roles, or scripts. Studies of mother-child social pretend play in the thirty-one to thirty-six-month period suggest that mothers move to a supportive rather than a directive role in play when the child begins to negotiate play.

The absence of studies on mother-child play negotiations in contrast to the plethora of studies on peer play negotiations suggests that mothers tend not to negotiate. The few studies of mother-child pretend play during this period suggest that the mother encourages the child to be independent in play rather than actively collaborating in the construction of play. See table 6.1. This does not mean, as we shall discuss further in this chapter, that adults, particularly parents, cease to influence social pretend play. In contrast, parent-child relationships and parental-child management style appear to be important influences on individual differences in a child's resolution of issues of control and compromise within peer play.

Social Competence and Social Pretend Play

The negotiation of social pretend play with peers requires many skills. Each child must formulate and express his or her play ideas so that the partner can understand his or her notions for roles and scripts. The child must attend to the partner's ideas for play. Finally, the child must participate in the coordination of play scripts and themes. If play is to be satisfying, each child must have opportunities to play out pretend themes that have individual meaning while simultaneously creating with a partner play that is free from disruptive disagreements. Thus, within social pretend play, children balance their individual needs to control the play with the necessity for compromise in order to play at all.

Given these requirements for play it is not surprising that several researchers assume a theoretical link between social pretend with peers and social competence with peers. Several empirical studies report associations between the frequency of social pretend play in preschool-age children and measures of social acceptance (Connolly & Doyle 1984; Rosenberg 1983). Social acceptance as measured through sociometric techniques is frequently used as a marker of social competence with preschool and older children (Hartup 1983; Howes 1988).

Developmental theorists speculate that the association between social pretend play and social competence with peers is due to the stimulation of cognitive processes through negotiation and enactment (Fein 1981; Garvey 1977; Rubin 1980; Rubin, Fein, & Vandenberg 1983). As the child negotiates and engages in social pretend play, he/she develops social-cognitive skills including social role understanding, conflict resolution, and, more generally, communicative competence. These social-cognitive skills are individual skills. However, most social pretend play is a dyadic product, usually of two well-acquainted children. Thus, the independent assessment of social competence and social pretend play has been problematic.

The independent assessment of social competence and social pretend play has been particularly problematic because social pretend play is usually constructed within well-established play groups and social competence is usually assessed with sociometric techniques. When these procedures are employed the association between social pretend play and social competence may have less to do with individual skills than with the fit of a particular child within a specified group of children. We suspect that children who are flexible and willing to compromise in their play negotiations and who cooperatively generate play ideas that have meaning to others are the children who are liked by the others. Flexibility in the generation of social problem-solving solutions is often considered a social cognitive skill (Rubin & Krasnor 1986). Unfortunately, the same child who generates many problem-solving solutions in an interview may, due to emotional rather than cognitive causes, be inflexible in real life situations (Rubin & Krasnor 1986). The child who is flexible in play negotiations and cooperatively generates play ideas fits the profile of a peer leader as described by LaFreniere and Sroufe (1985). Peer leadership is often seen as a consequence of secure caregiver attachments (LaFreniere & Sroufe 1985). Therefore, the reported relation between social pretend play and peer acceptance may be based on social-emotional rather than social-cognitive functioning.

A recent study by Doyle and Connolly (1989) provides support for this hypothesis. These researchers observed pretend play negotiations and enactments during free play periods in child care. They also assessed both peer acceptance (sociometric) and affective role taking. Frequency of pretend play enactment predicted peer acceptance independent of negotiation, but failed to predict peer acceptance. Neither frequency of pretend play enactment nor negotiation predicted affective role taking, an individual measure of social cognition. We suspect that those children who spent relatively long periods of time negotiating as opposed to playing pretend were also more likely to engage in peer conflict. Peer conflict is associated with lowered peer acceptance (Hartup 1989).

We further suspect that one reason for the lack of relation between affective role taking and social pretend play in the Connolly and Doyle study is because the frequency of social pretend play with familiar peers in a familiar setting is dependent, in part, on the children's histories of harmonious or disharmonious play. A child could be very skillful at affective role taking and still be disparate from the group in terms of play interests or styles. We could attempt test associations between the development of social cognition and social pretend play in individual children by observing the child in social pretend play with several unfamiliar partners and relating the play to measures of social cognition. This design would be useful for separating a child's individual skill in constructing play from the contribution of the relationship with the partner.

Harmonious Social Pretend Play Negotiations

Social pretend play themes. If at least part of the link between social pretend play and social competence is dependent on generating play ideas that have meaning to others, it is important to examine social pretend themes.

There is a small body of research on common themes of pretend play. Initially, children's social pretend centers around familiar domestic themes—housekeeping and caring for babies (Howes et al. 1989; Nelson & Seidman 1984). With wider experience in the community, children add themes such as fire fighting and transportation. Later in preschool, children elaborate "lost-found," "danger-rescue," and "death-rebirth" themes (Corsaro 1985). These age-appropriate concerns appeal to most children. We suspect that a child who refuses to engage in these common themes or who insists on idiosyncratic variations on the themes will be less accepted as a pretend play partner.

Flexible role negotiations.   Some roles in play are more desirable than others. For example, everyone wants to be the mother and no one wants to be the dog in a game of house. More popular children usually play the more desirable parts (Segal et al. 1987), but if a child is too insistent on playing a particular role he or she may become less accepted by peers. Sometimes a less popular child can become more popular by a creative and harmonious enactment of a less popular role. For example, one child new to the group gained peer acceptance through her enactment of the dog role in the house game. Therefore, through exploring autonomy, control, and compromise in social pretend play negotiations of themes, scripts, and role enactment, children learn how to both express their own concerns and to be a member of a social group.

Friendships.   Older preschool children who are friends have fewer disagreements and their pretend play is more harmonious than dyads who are not friends (Gottman 1986). Since in large-scale studies of children enrolled in child care only a small percentage of three-year-old children do not have reciprocated friends (Howes 1983; 1988), it is unlikely that only children who are particularly skilled at negotiating play become friends. A reciprocated friendship is a dyad in which each partner is selected as a friend by the other (Howes 1988).

It is more likely that friendships form on the basis of a match between social pretend play interests. Despite a growing literature on young friendships, there is little agreement or information on how particular children select each other as friends (Hartup 1989). Comparing the themes of the social pretend play of friends and acquaintances might be a fruitful direction for research in this area.

Children who are friends become very experienced at social play negotiations, and appear motivated to sustain less than pleasant negotiations perhaps because they know that the resulting play will be pleasurable. In illustrative study #4 we will discuss relations between friendship and intimacy themes in social pretend play. In the course of collecting data we recorded the following exchange between two three-and-a-half-year-old boys who had been enrolled in the same child-care center and friends since infancy. This excerpt illustrates how tenacious friends sometimes have to be during negotiations.

The children were asked to play at a table with a set of replica toys. There was one red motorcycle which George began playing with immediately upon sitting down. After about four minutes Kary says, "Let's trade."

G: No, I don't want to.

K: You gotta trade.

G: No, I don't have to if I don't want to (moves motorcycle and makes car noises).

K: I can trade if I want to.

G: Well, I don't have to.

K: I have to.

G: Well, I—.

K: You do and I do.

G: Huh.

K: If, if I do you do.

G: But I don't want to.

Eight minutes pass, George continues to play with the motorcycle and Kary continues to eye it. There is sporadic parallel play but no organized and coordinated play. George momentarily removes his hand from the motorcycle and Kary grabs it.

K: I've got this.

G: No.

K: I found it.

G: (In a whining voice) Give it to me.

K: I saw it.

G: Give it.

K: George.

G: (Reaches for the motorcycle) I want it back.

K: No.

G: (With trembling lip) Give it to me. (Sits back in his chair with arms crossed and a pouting face)

K: I saw it there, George, I saw it.

The two boys continue this dialogue for several minutes with George pouting and Kary sternly admonishing, "You've gotta share, George." Finally, Kary says, "Well, if you don't share I'm not going to play with you." George says, "Well you, I have an idea. How about I have this for a long time," looks at Kary's defiant face and continues, "A little bit longer, then I'll give it to you." He checks out Kary's face and says, "I'll just have it a little more longer and then I'll give it to you, ok?" Kary replies, "When the man falls off, how 'bout that?" and hands the motorcycle to George. George makes the man fall off the motorcycle five seconds later, hands the motorcycle to Kary, and the boys move into a coordinated fantasy. The turning point in this negotiation appeared to be when Kary threatened George with the loss of the friendship: "Well, if you don't share I'm not going to play with you." We suspect that both Kary and George knew how far to push the other without truly jeopardizing the relationship.

Friends might have more harmonious pretend play because they have a shared history. Children who become friends while enrolled in child care have often spent several years in intimate daily contact (Howes 1988). Likewise, children who become friends because their families are friends have a history of shared play experiences in several contexts. Negotiations would be less prolonged or intense when roles and basic scripts are at least partly decided in advanced. This could be very positive if such a shared notion of the play leaves room for complex variations and elaborations on basic themes and scripts. However, friendships do exist between dominant and subordinate children. In this type of friendship there might be little opportunity for play negotiation. Instead, one child would direct the pretend and the other would simply play his or her assigned role. Social pretend play in these "uneven" friendships may not function as a means for exploring issues of control and compromise nor would such social pretend play necessarily foster development (Rubin 1980).

The ethnographic writings of Paley (1986 1988) suggest that identifying "uneven" friendships is a difficult task, one that requires intensive and sensitive observation especially as social pretend play negotiation becomes a means of exploring the boundaries of friendships. Paley describes the friendship of Mollie and Christopher as three (1986) and as four-year-olds (1988). Originally, Mollie, who has had an easy adjustment to preschool, is the dominant child both in the friendship and in the negotiation of pretend. She is a major factor in helping Christopher, who has had a difficult transition to preschool, become a part of the peer group. Over time Christopher becomes more assertive within the friendship and the classroom.

"Okay," Mollie says, "You can be the baby and I'm the mother." "No. I'm the mother," Christopher states. "You can be the daddy. That's much nicer." "No, Mollie, I'm already being the mother. You can be the daddy . . . Or you could be the baby, Mollie." "Okay, I'll be the daddy," Mollie says. (Paley 1986, 131).

As four-year-olds the children remain friends and their play negotiations are smooth and balanced. Mollie and Christopher are playing in the doll corner. Christopher says,

"I finished sleeping. Now I have to go to work, mother." Mollie grabs his arm, "Don't go. Stay in bed with the baby. I'll wake you when the alarm clocks." "I got my tie on already. I saw the day. I'll be right back, Mollie." Mollie is upset. "Stay here, father, I hear a noise in the chimney." "Then it's the wolf," Christopher says, "I'll get the bullets." (Paley 1988, 2425)

Another boy enters the doll corner as the wolf and knocks over chairs, clawing at the dishes and playdough. The teacher intervenes,

Teacher: "Fredrick, really! Look at this mess. What are you playing?" "They said I'm the wolf." "He's a different wolf that got eated up," Mollie explains. She has already begun to reset the table. "Am I still the father, Mollie?" Christopher asks, "Are you my friend?" "I'm the both of your friend," she says, pressing out heart shaped cookies. "You can both come to my birthday." (Paley 1988, 2425)

Parents and social pretend play negotiations. There is general agreement within the field that the parent-child and child-child social systems are not totally independent. Therefore, even if mothers no longer play pretend with their children they could facilitate the child's mastery of autonomy and compromise within social pretend. There are currently no empirical studies that examine associations between maternal styles or techniques and children's individual differences in social pretend play competence with their peers, although researchers have long assumed that early parent use of make believe and the modeling of turn taking are critical for the development of pretend play (Singer 1973; Smilansky 1968). However, a growing literature supports the premise that parental behaviors may be associated with more competent play with peers. Parke and associates suggest that families influence peer relations through direct and indirect paths (Parke et al. in press). The family indirectly modifies or enhances peer relations as a result of the quality of the parent-child attachment relationships. From these attachment relationships the child forms a working model of the self and relations with others (Bretherton 1985).

Attachment Security

As we have reviewed, younger children with secure attachment relationships appeared competent in mother-child social pretend play (Slade 1987a). There currently are no studies that examine associations between maternal attachment and the child's social pretend play negotiations with peers. See illustrative study #5 for an exception. We expect that securely attached children would be better able to negotiate and compromise within play because their internal models of the self and other permit flexibility. We expect the secure child to feel sufficiently confident of being liked by others that they would be forceful in expressing his or her own play ideas yet simultaneously sufficiently positive in his or her view of the other to be agreeable to the partner's suggestions. Therefore, we would expect the securely attached child to both freely make autonomous play suggestions and to compromise with the partner. We expect an insecurely attached child to be less flexible and to either refuse to play anything except his or her self-generated pretend or to immediately acquiesce to all of the partner's suggestions and demands.

Parent-Child Play

The family may also indirectly influence peer relations through the quality of the parent-child play (Parke et al. in press). According to this thesis, when children play with their parents they learn the social communicative value of their own affective displays as well as how to use these signals to regulate the social behavior of others (Parke et al. in press). They may also learn to accurately decode the social and affective signals of other social partners (Parke et al. in press). These hypotheses have been tested for relations between parent-child play and peer relations in general. Preschool children whose parents engage with them in play and in particular elicit effect in their play are ranked as more accepted by their peers (MacDonald & Parke 1985; Parke et al. in press). Furthermore, children who frequently engage in physical play with their fathers are better able to correctly identify emotional states (Beitel & Parke 1985).

Again, there are no current studies that examine these hypotheses for social pretend play. We can speculate that if children have experience with decoding affective displays within parent-child play they would be better able to negotiate and compromise with peers in social pretend play because such negotiation and compromise rest on skillful social communication and affective decoding. If the play is to go on the child must determine if the emotion the partner is expressing is within or outside the play frame and if it threatens or enhances the play. For example, a child must distinguish between the partner who looks angry because she is the bad witch and the partner who looks angry because she doesn't want to be the bad witch.

Management of Children's Play

Parke and associates (Parke et al. in press) suggest that families also modify their children's peer relations directly. Families manage peer relations by their social arrangements and by monitoring and serving as "coaches" of peer contacts. See illustrative study #4. Variations in these management techniques appear related to the child's competence with peers. Ladd and Golter (1988) report that parents who actively arranged peer contacts had children with more extensive and consistent networks of peer partners. As discussed earlier, harmonious social pretend play, at least for younger and less socially skilled children, is associated with consistent play partners. Therefore, parents may directly influence thier child's competence in social pretend through providing frequent and consistent play partners.

Ladd and Golter (1988) also found relations between parent reports of their behaviors during peer contacts and their children's social adjustment in school. Parents who were more directive were more likely to have maladjusted children. Again, there are currently no studies that examine parental management style and social pretend play with peers, but the Ladd and Golter study suggests hypotheses for further study. Perhaps the same parents who direct the child's play with peers provide few opportunities for autonomous expression in the child. The child may understand that only one person can win in a conflict and be unwilling to compromise in pretend play negotiations.

Summary

In summary, we have suggested that social pretend play functions as an opportunity to explore issues of autonomy, control, and compromise during the early preschool period. Descriptive studies report that extensive play negotiations are normative during this period. We have suggested that the reported association between social competence and social pretend play during this period can be explained by social cognitive skills, the child's flexibility, and the fit between the concerns of the child and the concerns of the group. The children who can engage in more harmonious and complex social pretend play are considered the more socially competent. Further research is needed to define and extend our notions of the fit or match between the child and the group. Fruitful directions might include examining similar shared meanings and themes, similar, complementary, or discordant play styles, and the distribution of play roles.

While parents become less active in playing pretend with their children during this period, we have suggested that they continue to influence the child's social pretend play. In contrast with the previous section on mastery of social pretend play forms, this section on issues of control and compromise is more speculative. We hope that our speculations and hypotheses will lead to future research.

We have generated two illustrative studies to elaborate issues of control and compromise in play negotiations. These studies follow directly from speculations raised in this chapter about the role of parents in enhancing their children's social pretend play. Both direct and indirect parental influences are examined. Study #4, Mother's Beliefs About Mediating Peer Play and Toddler-Age Children's Peer Networks, begins the task of elucidating links between parents' management roles and their children's social pretend play. Study #5, Attachment Security and Social Pretend Play Negotiations, turns to intersections between relations within the family and behaviors within the peer group. In this study we describe and contrast the social pretend play negotiations of children with secure and insecure maternal attachments.

7

Mothers' Beliefs about Mediating Peer Play and Toddler-Age Children's Peer Networks: Illustrative Study #4

Olivia A. Unger

Within the literature there is a pervasive idea that the nature of peer relationships is dependent upon mother-child relationships (Halverson & Waldrop
1970; Cochran & Brassard 1979; Macoby & Martin 1983; Sroufe 1983;
Rubin & Sloman 1984; Hay 1985; Elias & Ubriaco 1986; Parke et al in press;
Whiting & Edwards 1988). Maternal influence on children's peer relationships has been described as occurring along two paths, namely indirect and
direct paths of influence (Parke et al. 1986; Parke & Bhavnagri 1988).

Mothers indirectly influence peer relationships through the quality of
the mother-child attachment relationship. Success in peer relationships is
believed to be an extension of the secure attachment achieved with the mother (Hay 1985 Parke et al. 1986). Researchers have found that the quality of
attachment in infancy predicts children's social competence in preschool
with peers (Arend, Gove, & Sroufe 1979; Waters, Wippman, & Sroufe 1979;
LaFreniere & Sroufe 1985; Jacobson & Wille 1986). Within this paradigm,
mothers influence peer relationships through generalization of the harmonious relationship and social skills developed in the context of the family
(Parke et al. in press).

Whereas the goal of indirect influences is not to explicitly modify or
enhance children's relationships with other children, the goal of direct maternal influences is to actively select, modify, or structure the environment to
facilitate peer relationships (Parke et al. in press). The concept of mothers as
managers of their children's social lives is a relatively recent notion within

the social development literature (Parke 1978; Hartup 1979; Ladd & Golter 1988). Functionally, the concept of mothers as managers describes mothers' dual roles as arrangers of peer opportunities and as supervisors of peer play. These dual roles encompass two broad sets of activities.

Recent research suggests that mothers exert a primary influence on determining the social network of young children (Ladd et al. 1988; Ladd & Golter 1988). In the context of arranging peer contacts, mothers bear a direct influence on their children's social relationships by determining the timing and circumstances of contact they will have with persons outside of the family. Mothers organize play groups or enroll their children in activities involving other children (Hartup 1979; Rubin & Sloman 1984; Ladd & Golter 1988; Parke & Bhavnagri 1988; Salzinger, Hammer, & Antrobus 1988; Salzinger & Hampson 1988). Mothers' initiation of contact with potential playmates is particularly important for young children who are not mobile or independent (Bhavnagri 1987; Parke & Bhavnagri 1988)

Children's social adjustment or competence has been found to be related to their social networks (see Cochran & Brassard 1979). Children's social networks consist of the people outside of the household with whom they are engaged in activities and interactions of an affective and/or material nature (Cochran & Brassard 1979). Contact with other children appears to enhance the communicative function of speech (Salzinger & Hampson 1988); decrease the likelihood of behavioral problems (Lewis et al. 1984); and increase social competence with peers (Howes 1988). It has been suggested that by twenty months of age children spend a significant amount of time with peers whether in child care (Howes 1988) or being cared for in the home (Salzinger & Hampson 1988). To date, there is an extremely limited literature that describes toddlers' social networks, and there is a need for the most basic kind of information such as what constitutes normal or adequate social contact for children (Salzinger, Antrobus, & Hammer 1988).

As managers of peer play, mothers also bear a direct influence on their children's peer relationships through their monitoring and supervision of peer activities. The concepts of monitoring and supervision reflect a range of maternal activities including the extent of supervision provided (Parke & Bhavnagri 1988). Aspects of parental management can assume a variety of forms and include such behaviors as watching closely or from a distance, guiding or joining play, helping to initiate interactions, sustaining interactions, responsiveness, and level of positive affect (Rubin & Sloman 1984; Parke et al. in press; Ladd & Golter 1988). Particular forms of supervision have been found to contribute to children's social competence at different points of development—that is, younger children require greater amounts of parental support to sustain competent peer interaction than older children (Parke & Bhavnagri 1988).

Although the literature has begun to address a range of activities that constitutes monitoring or supervision, the specific mediation strategies or tactics mothers use to directly assist children to initiate play, maintain interaction, and resolve conflicts has received only limited attention (Parke & Bhavnagri 1988). Only one previous study explored the relationship between parents' monitoring of preschoolers' peer contacts and the qualities of children's peer relationships in both nonschool and school settings (Ladd & Golter 1988). In this study, parental report measures were used to describe how peer contacts were initiated, who was the primary instigator, and how contact was monitored (e.g., by being present, participating in the activity, or watching). The results suggested that directive styles of parental supervision in nonschool settings were related to social maladjustment in school. However, no relationship was found between indirect or direct forms of parental monitoring and the nonschool peer relations of the children. Although the results found by Ladd and Golter (1988) suggest that aspects of parenting are related to children's social competence, there are two important limitations of their study. First, by utilizing a parental report measure, the authors may have described the mothers' perceptions or beliefs about their monitoring behavior rather than their actual behaviors. Second, although this research suggests that aspects of parenting may be related to success in peer relationships, the reasons why mothers applied particular forms of peer mediation remains unclear. That is, mothers may have particular beliefs or values regarding how to guide their children's peer interactions that may influence their use of particular mediation strategies (Rubin & Sloman 1984). Ladd and Golter (1988) comment that the children who display higher social competence may require less parental supervision than those children with interpersonal difficulties. What is not known is whether the mothers actually perceived differences in the children.

Thus, past research suggests a relationship between aspects of maternal behavior and children's peer relationships. Yet, the mechanisms regulating maternal behavior are not well understood. Investigators have found that maternal behavior may be regulated in part by maternal beliefs. There is a growing body of literature on parental beliefs about developmental processes and specific abilities and their effects on children's development (Miller 1988). However, the focus of this work has been predominantly to predict children's cognitive development.

The definition of social competence used in the present study is from the work of Howes (1987, 1988). Social competence with peers is defined as "behavior that reflects successful social functioning with peers" (Howes 1987, 253). Although numerous investigators (Asher & Gottman 1981; Hartup 1983; Dodge 1985) have examined the general construct of social competence with school-age children, it is only quite recently that developmental indices of social competence with peers have been addressed within the toddler period (Howes 1985 1987 1988; Howes, Unger, Seidner 1989). There are two central attainments representing competent social interaction with peers during the toddler period. A child's ability to engage in social interaction with a *complementary and reciprocal structure* is the central attainment of the early toddler period (13–24 months). Within such an interaction structure, peer partners exchange both turns and roles in action; that is, they engage in different but complementary activities such as run-and- chase, hide-and-seek, and offer and receive. The complementary role of the partner does not require children to communicate the meaning of their actions. During the late toddler period (25–36 months), *communication of meaning* defined as the "joint understanding of the theme of the interaction" represents the central attainment of the socially competent child (Howes 1988, 3). A child's ability to engage in social pretend play has been proposed as the operational definition of communication of meaning (Howes 1987). In order to engage in social pretend play, children must integrate nonliteral pretense meanings into their complementary and reciprocal social interaction (Howes 1985). Cooperative social pretend play is the most advanced form of social pretend play to emerge during the late toddler period. Cooperative social pretend requires the children to communicate that they have assumed complementary pretend roles such as mommy and baby and understand that their partner is acting out a role (Howes 1987, 1988). Research to date has examined social pretend play with peers separately from the adult-child social system.

Variations in peer experience have been found to influence the development of social pretend play. For toddlers, experience with peers in a stable peer group facilitates socially competent behavior. Early toddler-age children who had been in a stable peer group for more than one year were found to engage in more complementary and reciprocal play and were rated by teachers as having less difficulty with peers than children who had spent less time in peer groups. For older toddlers, children with more experience were found to engage in more cooperative social pretend and had less difficulty with peers (Howes 1988). In a commentary of the Howes (1988) study, Rubin and Ross proposed that examination of maternal beliefs and strategies may also predict individual differences in children's social pretend play. The ways in which parents view their children's social behavior with peers is important because it may influence the way they interact with their children and consequently their children's social competence. Children do not have direct access to their mothers' beliefs but develop expectancies about their parents' behavioral standards through the strategies used by their parents in interpersonal situations over time (Elias & Ubriaco 1986).

In this chapter, a preliminary examination of data from a larger study of mothers' beliefs about the strategies they use when mediating their children's peer play is made. The purpose of the present study is twofold. First, to describe mothers' beliefs about two specific peer behaviors, sharing and initiating play. These are social behaviors identified by practitioners as important aspects of peer socialization during the toddler developmental period (Gurian & Formanek 1983). In addition, sharing and initiation of play may be strategies used by toddlers to attain the marker behaviors of social competence identified by Howes (1987, 1988). For example, sharing a toy may be one manner in which children begin to engage in "complementary and reciprocal play"; initiating play may be a means of communicating a joint-play theme.

The second purpose is to describe the peer network of the children. Since young children are dependent upon mothers for arranging and mediating peer contacts, toddler age children were the focus of the present study. In addition, toddler-age children were chosen because of the limited amount of research conducted with this age group, and the potential significance of the peer network in the development of social competence (Howes 1987; Ladd et al. 1988).

Method

Subjects

Eight Caucasian mothers and their children from affluent socioeconomic backgrounds were recruited through word of mouth contacts, local toddler programs, and gym classes in the Los Angeles area. The mothers ranged in age from 27 to 37 years (Mdn = 32). Three of the mothers work twenty to forty hours per week and five were unemployed. All children came from two-parent families where both parents have college degrees. There were four boys and four girls in the group of children; all were firstborn. The children ranged in age from twenty-five to thirty months of age.

Instruments

Peer social network: telephone interviews and logs. Following the method developed by Ladd and Golter (1988), telephone interviews were conducted with the mothers in order to compile a record of the children's peer contacts for four weekdays and either a Saturday or Sunday. The mothers were asked to "Think of the day as divided into three blocks of time: morning, afternoon, and evening. For each of these time periods, tell me the hours _____ (name of child) spent with a peer." For each reported occurrence of peer contact the mother was asked to describe how the contact had been initiated, who had been the primary instigator (e.g., the parent initiated it, the child asked to see a particular peer), the location of the contact (e.g., the child's house, playmate's house, or other locations), and how often they see each other. Intervals that children spent with peers in toddler classes or child-care settings were also recorded. For recording purposes, the beginning and end of a contact was defined as the cessation of play, or by changes in play locations or partners (e.g., a new peer joins the activity).

The mothers were also asked if during the course of the week there were regularly scheduled activities or visits with peers. For example, one mother reported that her child attends a toddler group for two hours every Monday morning by himself and on Tuesday and Thursday afternoons plays with a neighborhood friend in the presence of both mothers.

Maternal beliefs vignettes. The mothers were verbally presented with two vignettes about sharing and initiating play. Each vignette was followed by a series of probe questions. All responses were tape recorded and conducted with the mothers in the privacy of their own homes. The interview sessions were approximately 20–30 minutes long. The vignettes were introduced in the following manner, "I will be reading you two short vignettes having to do with a child's sharing and initiating play with a friend. I would like you to answer by explaining what you would do if such a situation happened with your child." McGuillicudy-DeLisi (1985) and Sigel (1986) suggest that the parent be oriented toward the behavior of their own child rather than other children in general in order to facilitate the belief-behavior link. Following this suggestion, the vignettes use the name of the mother's child and same-sex peer. In addition, information regarding the family's demographic characteristics was obtained.

Results and Discussion

Peer Network

Data from the telephone interviews and logs revealed considerable variability in the number of contacts children had with peers over the sampled interval. Peer contact was defined as an activity or series of activities continuously performed by the child with one or more children outside of regularly scheduled classes or groups attended (adapted definition from Ladd and Golter 1988). The number of peer contacts reported by parents across the five days of data gathering ranged from 1 to 12 for the entire sample (Mdn = 2.5), from 1 to 12 for boys (Mdn = 8) and from 1 to 4 for girls (Mdn = 2.5). The mothers initiated from 0 to 66 percent of all peer contacts. The remainder of peer contacts were initiated by the peers' mothers or requested by the children themselves. In addition to the peer contacts, the children attended from one to three regularly scheduled classes or groups per week. These groups included music and art classes, gym, "Mommy and me," or preschool transition programs that were led by an instructor and contained a combination of free play and structured activities. With the exception of the preschool transition programs, the mothers were present and participated in the activities. Previous studies have provided some evidence that upper-middle-class families are more likely to participate in prearranged and structured social interactions than working-class families who were more attuned to spontaneous interactions (Berg & Medrich 1980).

In addition, three of the mothers reported participating in a weekly play group where five to six children and their mothers meet at each other's homes. These are informal groups that are loosely structured whereby the children play with toys while their mothers socialize. Consistent with previous research, parents often arranged contacts between their children and the children of their own friends because the contacts were easy to arrange and they themselves wanted to spend time together (Rubin & Sloman 1984). Parents reported that they were often not directly involved in their children's play but arranged or suggested toys for the children to play with and intervened when conflicts arose.

Maternal Beliefs

In order to categorize the data from the beliefs vignettes, a content analysis was performed. The derived categories reflect the mothers' conceptualization as to why they utilize particular strategies to facilitate their children's sharing and initiation of play. The categories are not mutually exclusive. Mothers were found to simultaneously hold multiple beliefs. The context in which a problem with sharing or initiation of play occurred appeared to be a critical variable in determining the strategy mothers would use. Contextual factors considered important by the mothers were whether the children were familiar with one another, who had the toy first, whether a similar toy was available, and whether the other mother was present.

Sharing. Five categories of beliefs regarding sharing were found.

1. *Children need external rules to help them take turns.* Parents would use such techniques as counting to twenty, using a real or imaginary timer, or would model how to physically trade toys with a peer and then verbally ask for the toy back.

"It just seems like it's more concrete. It's not that I'm taking the toy away. It's not like Jordan is taking the toy away. It's just that your time is up when the buzzer is up."

2. *Children have the right to "not share" and the other child should be expected to wait.* Parents felt that whomever had the toy first was entitled to play with it and expected the other child to wait his or her turn.

"Cause I really feel when one child, especially at this age, is in the midst of playing with something it is their's to play with and they have the right to continue playing with it and not just because another child wants to play with it to give it up. If they choose to, that is wonderful. At two years old, I just really don't believe it is necessary to insist that they part with it."

3. *Children should be encouraged to share but work it out for themselves.* Parents commonly would not intervene unless one of the children was crying.

"Because I think independence is a virtue, I want for Molly to work things out on her own and I want for her to learn. If I always intervene, then when I am not there she will not know what to do."

4. *Children can be distracted. One object can be substituted for another when both children want the same toy.* Parents would attempt to get their child interested in something else or offer a similar toy.

"Well, because they'll forget easily at this age what it was that they wanted if you can catch their attention."

5. *Sometimes children are unable to share and the toy should be removed.* Parents commonly responded that if the fighting over a desired object escalated between the two children that it should be removed. One parent commented that if the toy was very special it was to be put away when another child was visiting.

"If it is causing that much stress I usually say, 'Nobody gets the shovel and it gets put away because you are not learning how to cooperate today.'"

Initiating play. Three categories of maternal beliefs will be described along with illustrations. The mothers' assessment as to the degree of familiarity their child had with the peer seemed to determine the strategy used when helping their child initiate play. According to one parent, "When children know each other they know how to deal with each other, they know what the kid's toys are like. What their room is like It's just some familiarity, some sameness."

1. *When children know each other they do not need help playing with one another.* Parents described orienting the children to their toys and the children then going off to play on their own.

"You don't have to do a lot to get kids to play, they just do it. You don't have to say, 'Why don't you play with this or that?' Just have an area for them to play in. They'll just hang out or do whatever."

2. *When less familiar or reticent to interact, children need help getting it going.* Parents reported asking their child to show the other child a specific toy or setting up a turn-taking structure that encouraged the children to interact with one another.

"If they are holding on to their mother, then I introduce toys to get them involved with Ryan, or I say, 'Ryan, why don't you show them this?'

3. *Children do not know how to make friends and need instruction.*

"The kids need to learn how to make friends, it's not something that comes naturally. They learn to say, 'My name is Amy. Want to see my toys?'"

Conclusion

The preliminary data presented demonstrates several points. First, toddler-age children are frequently in the company of peers, whether it be during individual playtime with a peer, small groups, or in formal programs. Parents made considerable efforts to ensure their children had the opportunity to interact with their peers. Opportunities for peer interaction may allow for greater opportunity to acquire and practice socially skilled behavior and more complex forms of peer play (Doyle, Connolly, & Rivest 1979; Howes & Unger 1989). In order to further our understanding and description of children's peer networks we must consider family structure, situational factors and cultural variables that may constrain and shape children's social development along with the developmental status of the child.

Mothers' beliefs concerning social behaviors relevant to their toddler-age children's social competence were described and illustrated. Maternal beliefs about sharing and initiating play are presumed to bear an influence on the ways parents guide and control their children's peer relationships. The preliminary categories provided may be useful for organizing and examining why parents utilize particular mediation strategies with their children and their peers. These preliminary findings suggest that the strategies used by mothers develop as a function of the mothers' interactions with their children in a number of peer contexts and that situational factors influence the mothers' adherence to particular beliefs. While a link between what mothers think about their children's peer interactions and how they behave toward them has been proposed, future research on this issue seems critical toward our understanding of the relationship between beliefs and behavior.

8

Attachment Security and Social Pretend Play Negotiations: Illustrative Study #5

Carollee Howes and Carol Rodning

Attachment theory predicts that children who have established secure attachments to caregivers will have a positive orientation toward other social relationships (Bretherton 1985; Main, Kaplan, & Cassidy 1985). Peer relationships and particularly social pretend play with peers represent a stringent test of this hypothesis. Social interaction with a peer, particularly if the dyad engages in social pretend play, requires that both partners accommodate their behaviors to the other in order to achieve coordinated play. A successful and coordinated adult-child interaction will occur if the child makes little or no accommodation to the adult but the adult partner accommodates to the child's behavior. For example, a child might be able to initiate and sustain contact with an adult using minimal signals and paying minimal attention to the adult's responses because the adult, as a more expert communicator, is able to provide a scaffold for the child's inept behavior. Peers are less adept social players, and thus are less capable of providing a scaffold for the behavior of the partner.

Two criteria must be met before a peer dyad can successfully engage in social pretend play. The children must be willing to play with each other and they must communicate and coordinate individual nonliteral meanings. We expect children with insecure attachment relationships with caregivers to have more difficulty in meeting these criteria than children with secure attachment relationships with caregivers.

Children who have insecure attachment relationships with adult caregivers may be unwilling to engage in play. Initially, they may withdraw from

89

peer encounters, expecting other children to be hostile or unresponsive. Children who initially withdraw from peers may later be unable to successfully engage with peers because many social skills important for peer interaction are acquired within the context of peer contact. Very young children appear to use mutually enjoyable activities to structure simple social peer encounters such as offering and receiving objects, playing run-chase, or alternating jumping (Eckerman, Davis, & Didow 1989; Eckerman & Didow 1989; Howes 1988; Nadel & Fontaine 1989). Simple social encounters provide a framework for the development of more complex interaction with peers including social pretend play (Howes 1987, 1988). Therefore, a child who is unwilling to engage with peers not only does not engage in pretend play but may not have the social interaction skills to easily engage in social pretend play.

Alternatively, children with insecure attachments may engage with peers instead of withdrawing but may be unable to successfully negotiate harmonious play. Such a child may approach peers with the assumption that he or she will be mistreated by peers. To avoid this expected mistreatment the child may unconsciously decide to agree before being aggressed upon or may misinterpret friendly initiations, acting as if they were hostile. Aggressive behavior and misinterpretations of friendly initiations will interfere with the process of communicating and coordinating individual, nonliteral meanings. Children with insecure attachment histories may attempt to play pretend but find that they can not agree on the assignment of roles. Children who are prone to aggressive behaviors and to misinterpretation of the other's behavior may not be sufficiently flexible to sustain social pretend play. In contrast, we expect securely attached children to negotiate and compromise within play because he or she feels confident of being liked by others and therefore able to both express their ideas and attend to the suggestions of the other.

The study of individual differences in social pretend play negotiations can be informed by a recent and growing literature on children's conflicts in general (Shantz 1987). Conflicts are defined, not as aggressive encounters, but episodes in which children disagree. Thus, two children who are willing to play pretend together but are in disagreement about role assignment, script, or enactment are in conflict. Children who are friends are more articulate about their disagreements, and to compromise when there are conflicts (Gottman 1983). It is important to note that it is the manner of negotiating conflict rather than the presence or absence of disagreement that distinguished successful relationships (friendships) from less successful ones (acquaintances) (Hartup 1989; Hartup et al.1988). Furthermore, children able to sustain social interaction prior to a conflict are more likely than children who begin their engagement with a conflict to resolve the conflict and continue playing together (Laursen & Hartup 1989).

If we consider social pretend play negotiations a special case of conflict we expect that children who are successful at negotiation and mainte-nance of play will be able to more clearly articulate their nonliteral mean-ings, to compromise in the sharing of the fantasy script and enactments, and to continue the social pretend play following a disagreement. If attachment history does shape the child's expectations and interpretations of the behav-iors of the partner, and the child's capacity for flexibility in adjusting behav-ior to the partner, then we expect children with differing attachment histories to behave differently when faced with conflict. We expected children with insecure attachment histories to be more reluctant to engage in social pretend play than children with secure attachment histories. Furthermore, we expect-ed the play of children with insecure attachment histories to be easily dis-rupted by conflict, and for these children to have difficulty in negotiating a compromise and maintaining play following a conflict.

We tested these hypotheses using a sample of three-year-old children, part of a larger, longitudinal study of children between infancy and preschool. The children participated in the Ainsworth Strange Situation (Ainsworth et al. 1978) as infants and were observed with peers in preschool as three-year-olds. The social pretend play of children with secure versus insecure attachment histories was compared. We were particularly interested in whether children engaged in social pretend play, in conflicts or disruptions within social pretend play, and whether or not social pretend play was sus-tained over a relatively long period of time.

Method

Sample

Forty children (twenty girls), their mothers, and their preschool class-mates participated in the study. The children were part of a larger, longitudi-nal sample. We selected this subsample of forty children because they entered a child-care arrangement that included peers when they were older than thirty-two months and prior to their fourth birthdays. The children were all from middle-class families and were predominantly Euro-American in ethnic background. As three-year-olds they attended full and part-day preschool programs an average of twelve (ranged = 4 to 48) hours per week.

Procedures and Measures

Attachment classifications. All children were seen in a standard Ainsworth Strange Situation at twelve months of age. The children were classified according to standard procedures. Thirty of the children in the sample were classified as secure, and ten as insecure (6 A, 3 C, and 1 D).

Social pretend play. Each child was observed on two separate occasions by two different observers for 15 minutes per observation (total of 60 minutes of observations). Observations were divided into 5-minute blocks. Within each block the observers coded 15 continuous 20-second intervals.

Within each interval the observers coded the children's initiations and responses to initiations, the children's aggressive, conflictual, and prosocial behaviors, and their level of social and social pretend play. Interobserver reliability on these measures met or exceeded the criterion of kappa = .85. For the purposes of the current analysis, transcripts of social pretend play episodes were prepared from the code sheets. An episode began with initiation either from the target or from a potential partner and ended when an interval containing social pretend play was followed by an interval containing no social pretend play. *Social pretend play* was defined as at least parallel (Howes 1985; Howes et al. 1989). In *parallel social pretend play,* children engaged in similar pretend actions while simultaneously engaged in social exchange. Only those episodes containing at least one interval of social pretend play were analyzed.

The social pretend play transcripts were coded for the following measures: the *number* of social pretend play episodes; the *length* of each episode (the number of intervals from initiation to termination), and *embedded conflicts.* Embedded conflicts were defined as episodes that contained at least one of the following events: an initiation by the target child was rebuffed (the potential partner explicitly refused to play, ignored the initiation, or walked away); an initiation by a potential partner was rejected (the target child ignored the initiation, aggressed toward the initiator, or explicitly refused to play); play began but was interrupted by a verbal conflict, an object struggle, or physical aggression. Embedded conflicts could end the episode (the interval that contained the embedded conflict was the terminating interval) or be located at the beginning or the middle of an episode. Intercoder reliability on the coding of transcripts met or exceeded the criterion of kappa = .85.

Results

Social Pretend Play Episodes

Twenty-nine (73 percent) of the children engaged in at least one episode of social pretend play. Children with secure attachment histories were more likely to engage in social pretend play than children with insecure attachment histories ($\chi^2(1) = 9.40$, $p = .002$). The distribution of children with varying attachment histories who engaged in social pretend play is presented in table 8.1. Two children classified as "A" and one child classified as "C" engaged in social pretend play. Children with insecure attachment histories also engaged in fewer social pretend play episodes than children with secure attachment histories. The description of social pretend play episodes of children with secure and insecure attachment histories is presented in table 8.2.

Table 8.1   Attachment Security and Social Pretend Play

	NO EPISODES	ANY EPISODES
Secure	4	26
Insecure	7	3

Table 8.2   Differences in Social Pretend Play Episodes by Attachment Security of Child

	ATTACHMENT		
	Secure	Insecure	t
Social pretend play			
Number of episodes	4.1	.8	4.38***
Length in intervals of longest episode	4.6	1.4	2.48**

Length of Social Pretend Play Episodes

The length of a social pretend play episode is an indication of how well children are able to sustain social pretend play. The median length of a social pretend play episode in this sample was three units or one minute. Twenty (67 percent) of the children with secure attachment histories and two (20 percent) of the children with insecure attachment histories engaged in social pretend play episodes that lasted for one minute or more. Most (63 percent) of the social pretend play episodes of the children with insecure attachment histories who did engage in social pretend play were less than one minute long.

The longest two social pretend play episodes in this sample each lasted for thirteen units or over 4 minutes. Children with secure attachment histories had longer longest play episodes than children with insecure attachment histories. See table 8.2. The average longest play episode of children with secure attachment histories was over a minute and a half while the average longest play episode for children with insecure attachment histories was less than half a minute long.

Conflicts Embedded Within Social Pretend Play

Eleven (8 percent) of the 131 pretend play episodes contained an embedded conflict. table 8.3 compares embedded conflicts within the social pretend play of children with secure and insecure attachment histories. These embedded conflicts were disproportionately found in the social pretend play of children with insecure attachment histories. Almost twice as many children with insecure attachment histories who engaged in social pretend play had embedded conflicts as did children with secure attachment histories who engaged in social pretend play. More than three times as many of the social pretend episodes of children with insecure attachment histories contained embedded conflicts as did the social pretend episodes of children with secure attachment histories.

Table 8.3 Comparison of Secure and Insecure Children's Embedded Conflicts

| | ATTACHMENT | |
	Secure	Insecure
Percentage of children who engaged in social pretend play and had an embedded conflict	37	67
Percentage of social pretend play episodes containing an embedded conflict	7	25
Percentage of children in which an embedded conflict ended the social pretend play	20	100
Percentage of social pretend play episodes with embedded conflicts in which an embedded conflict ended the social pretend play	33	100

An embedded conflict does not necessarily mean that the dyad is unable to sustain social pretend play. Reasonable children can and do disagree about the course of the play. However, for all of the children with insecure attachment histories whose social play contained embedded conflicts and for all their episodes of social pretend play with embedded conflict, conflict did indeed end the play. This is in sharp contrast to the children with secure attachment histories. For only 20 percent of the children with secure attachment histories, and one-third of their social pretend play episodes with embedded conflict did the conflict end the play.

Discussion

Our findings support our hypotheses. Children with insecure attachment histories were less likely to engage in social pretend play than children with secure attachment histories. When children with insecure attachment histories did play pretend with a peer the episodes were shorter and more likely to contain embedded conflicts than the pretend play of children with secure attachment histories. Thus, the children with insecure attachment histories had difficulty in initiating and maintaining social pretend play.

These data must be taken as suggestive given the small sample size, especially of children with insecure attachment histories who engaged in social pretend play. However, they do raise questions for further research. For example, did the children with insecure attachment histories have low frequencies of social pretend play because they avoided other children and engaged in solitary behavior? Or did children with insecure attachment histories engage in aggressive behaviors that frightened off potential partners? Future researchers might videotape naturally occurring social pretend play among children with different attachment histories in order to better understand the processes involved in successful and unsuccessful social pretend play negotiations.

Part III

TRUST AND INTIMACY

9

Exploring Issues of Intimacy and Trust Within Social Pretend Play: A Review

By the end of the preschool period and continuing until middle childhood, children's social pretend play assumes the function of exploring issues of intimacy and trust. Social pretend play can only function as a mechanism for exploring intimacy and trust once children become expert players. We found ten studies in our literature search that described social pretend play in these oldest, most expert players. See table 9.1. By the time children are four or five they can easily switch between the literal and the nonliteral and have mastered the strategies of negotiation and compromise. Their play is extremely complex with roles and partners well integrated. Of course, there are individual differences in children's social pretend play interests, skills, and their flexibility and willingness to compromise with partners (Fein 1987).

Social Pretend Play with Friends and Playmates

We suspect that social pretend play does not function as a means for exploring intimacy and trust with all potential partners. Instead, during this period we see an intimate association between social pretend play and friendship. Young friendships are reciprocated relationships. Each partner selects the other as a friend and the play of the friends includes shared positive affect (Howes 1983, 1988).Friendship and social pretend play are linked in several different ways. The content of social pretend play may be important in the selection of friends. Children may select each other as friends if they have similar social pretend play interests. For example, a friendship may form over an interest in pretending to be pirates or ballet dancers. Social pretend play also is important in the process of forming and maintaining friend-ships (Gottman 1983), and children may use it to find common issues and a basis for friendship. Several researchers find that play between friends is qualitatively different than play between acquaintances (Gottman & Parkhurst 1980; Roopnarine & Field 1984). Friends have longer play episodes and are more likely to play in a harmonious fashion.

Table 9.1   Exploring Issues of Intimacy and Trust Within Social Pretend Play

	PARTNER	
Adult	Older Sib	Peer

49–65 months

		Play has an integrative structure of differ-ential roles. The roles are discussed and assigned, enacted interactively, and the role behavior of each partner continuously influences the other. New information is added to play scripts during pretend.[a]

[a] Doyle & Connolly 1989; Connolly, Doyle & Reznick 1988; Field, et al. 1982; Genishi 1983; Goncu 1987; Iwanaga 1973; Mathews 1977; Nelson & Seidman 1984; Pellegrini 1985; Sachs, et al. 1984.

Furthermore, Parker and Gottman (1989) suggest that social pretend play between friends is a form of self-disclosure. Younger children use social pretend play with friends to communicate information about themselves that they do not yet have the cognitive and linguistic sophistication to communi-cate during gossip or intimate talks. Through actions on objects and talking for objects children can communicate information that is too complex to dis-cuss without props. For example, children might structure a sequence in pre-tend where two bears become friends, have a fight, and resolve the fight. In this way they can convey information about friendship that they do not yet have the conceptual skills and vocabulary to discuss in an abstract fashion. Self-disclosure is a way to explore issues of trust and intimacy. We suggest that social pretend play between friends is qualitatively different because friends use self-disclosure within the play to achieve intimacy and trust. See illustrative study #6 for an elaboration of this point.

Children who are expert social pretend players still engage in it with playmates as well as friends. Preschool children spend more total time play-ing with acquaintances in child care than they do friends (Howes 1988). This disparity is presumably because the number of friends is very small relative to acquaintances and friends are not always available. For unacquainted children some pretend play themes are sufficiently universal that they can be used as "ice-breakers," or ways to start joint play (e.g., "Want to play house?). Limited self-disclosure, especially when it points out similarities, may also be used to initiate play with a playmate or nonacquaintance (e.g., "I have a dress just like yours"). However, as we will elaborate in the next section, we suspect that friends rather than playmates more often use social pretend play to achieve intimacy and trust.

Pretend Play as Self-Disclosure

If pretend play is an expression of the affective issues particular to the child (Fein 1985), then it represents an opportunity for children to work through major concerns and fears with another person. Therefore, social pretend play can be a form of self-disclosure. Through play the child reveals his or her central fears and concerns to the partner. When children express affective issues within play they are simultaneously exploring issues of intimacy and trust. They are testing the partner's reaction to their concerns and fears. For example, if a child wants to play "being afraid of the dark" and the partner agrees and builds on the script, the children have shared their fears and found them to strike a responsive cord in the other. On the other hand, if the partner says something like "Only babies are afraid of the dark, let's play that the daddy hits the mommy and the police come," the two children may be each using social pretend play to express fears and concerns, though their fears are so disparate that the play may fail to build trust and intimacy.

Parker and Gottman (1989) suggest social pretend play has high potential for reward as well as high potential for conflict. Play proceeds smoothly only if the partners are comfortable with each other and when they are willing to share themes and play scripts. If one partner's manner of expression or affective issue creates discomfort in the other partner, the play is unlikely to continue. Therefore, within play children explore what kinds of feelings may be expressed, in what context, and with which partner.

Friends, Self-Disclosure, and Social Pretend Play

Within the larger peer group children may select play partners with similar fears or concerns and this may become the basis for a friendship. Despite a growing literature on friendships between young children (see Gottman & Mettetal 1986; Howes 1988; and Parker & Gottman 1989, for reviews), relatively little is known about how particular children select each other as friends. One ethnographic study (Z. Rubin 1980) describes several friendships within a preschool classroom. Each friendship, although different in many ways from the others, was characterized by common interests, compatible play styles, and enjoyment in the company of the other. Although Rubin does not describe the social pretend play of each pair of friends, we suspect that the common interests of the friends extended to social pretend play themes or that common interests and fears led to the joint creation of shared themes.

Paley's ethnographic work (1984, 1986, 1988) does provides descriptions of children's social pretend play and friendships. She provides many excellent examples of the integration of one child's particular interests and concerns into the pretend themes of the group. For example, Fredrick's mother has just had a new baby—a fact that upsets Fredrick and that he has refused to discuss with his teacher. Instead, Fredrick attempts to take the role of a newborn baby in every pretend play. Sometimes this role is tolerated:

> "I'm both of your baby cat, Meow, meow. I want my milk now." Fredrick lies down on the floor. Margaret smiles. "Mommy will come. Here kitty, your bottle." "We're not playing baby, Fredrick," Margaret tells him abruptly. (Paley 1988, 54)

Often the baby role is resisted:

> "Ma-ma." "Stop that, Fredrick," Mollie warns. "No babies. We didn't have our babies yet." (Paley 1988, 60)

Following multiple repetitions of the baby role, Fredrick transforms himself into first a mother:

> "Hey, Mollie, y'wanna see my bear? I'm building him a house big enough for him to sit or lay down. See this football shirt he's wearing? I weared it when I was baby." (Paley 1988, 74)

And then into a hunter:

> "I'll be right back, mother. I have to hunt for a lion for our supper. The baby is hungry for lion meat." (Paley 1988, 77)

In the process he returned to his leader role in the group. We suspect that Fredrick could play out his "baby" concerns because of his preexisting friendship within the group and because he used an acceptable way of expressing distress. His friendship ties presumably led his peers to be tolerant of aberrant behavior. If Fredrick had chosen to express his unhappiness about the new baby in aggressive angry play he might have been rejected. By using social pretend play to express distress he was able to remain within the peer group and work through his problem.

A content analysis of the social pretend play of friends might be a productive direction to examine as we attempt to understand the basis for attraction between children. Gottman's work is noteworthy in this area. He has recorded and transcribed the conversations of friends across childhood. These conversations of friends suggest that the social pretend play of friends is harmonious (Gottman & Mettetal 1986; Parker & Gottman 1989). The play of friends includes relatively high levels of agreement and involves complex coordination. Gottman (1986) also cites examples of friends who use fantasy to work out common fears (e.g., of the dark).

We do not yet know if children become friends because they share interests and affective issues. We know that children who are becoming friends attempt to define themselves as being similar rather than different (Parker & Gottman 1989). Once children begin to define themselves as friends, the friendship appears to provide a secure base for self-disclosure within social pretend play. This self-disclosure is a means of exploring trust and intimacy. Through these experiences of intimacy and trust the children build and develop their friendships.

Self-disclosure within social pretend play can potentially influence friendship in several ways. Some children may become friends because of a common affective issue (e.g., divorce). Within their social pretend play they may repeatedly explore themes such as abandonment or interpersonal hostility. Once the children have resolved their concerns they may end their friendship. Perhaps the joint play was important but the pair failed to resolve issues of trust and intimacy. Other children may become friends with a shared affective concern, explore their fears in play, and remain friends as their interests change with their development. For example, two ten-year-old girls, friends for five years, transformed their familiar "caring for the babies" pretend play script into a script that included getting a baby-sitter, going out, and talking about dating and other teenage activities. In this case the exploration of trust and intimacy within the early social pretend play was sufficiently satisfying to perpetuate the friendship and allow them to explore new concerns. In a third example, children may become friends, use social pretend play to express fears or concerns and experience intimacy and trust, and then an external event may provide one child with a fear or concern that is not shared. In some friendships the friend is able to provide support even when he or she does not share the concern. In other cases the friendship dies (e.g., "She was in that stupid car accident and now all she wants to play is hospital"). We need careful qualitative and descriptive research to explore interrelationships between social pretend play content, self-disclosure, and trust within the play and friendships.

Adults and the Trust and Intimacy Functions
of Social Pretend Play

We suspect that issues of trust and intimacy are not only explored within peer social pretend play. Parents and children may still play pretend. In one of our families many of the nine-year-old daughter's dolls and stuffed animals have names and personalities and are used by both parents and the child to act out variations on social pretend play scripts. For example, a seal has to be watched very carefully or she will run away and play in the bathtub. A doll frequently decides to do tricks at bedtime instead of settling down to sleep. The function of this social pretend play appears to be fun and connectedness.

Parents may indirectly influence the child's use of play to explore intimacy and trust within friendships. As we have discussed earlier, the parent-child attachment relationship may serve as a working model for peer relationships. We suspect that the securely attached child will find it easier than the anxiously attached child to use self-disclosure and build trust within friendships. See illustrative study #7. Children whose parents are integrated into social networks themselves may be more likely to build their own friendship networks. If the parents have placed a positive value on friends then they are likely both to communicate this to the child and to provide opportunities for the child that foster friendship. In addition, the parent's network of friendships is likely to include children who are potential friends for the child. There is a need for more research to examine relations between parent-child relationships, family patterns of social support, and children's experiences building trust and intimacy within friendships.

Social Adjustment and Social Pretend Play

Bretherton (1987) argues that only in well-adjusted, secure children does social pretend play function as an opportunity for emotional mastery. She bases this argument in large part on Rosenberg's work on attachment security and social pretend play themes and enactments. Rosenberg (1983) found that children classified as securely attached to their mothers in the Ainsworth Strange Situation at eighteen months engaged in qualitatively different pretend play as four-year-olds than children classified as insecure. The securely attached children had more theme elaboration, and social flexibility. Their play more often involved positive themes, combined positive and negative affect, and contained benign resolutions of pretend problems. In contrast, the play of the children classified as insecure more often contained aggressive and generally unpleasant themes, expressions of anger, and unresolved problems. Bretherton suggests that the insecurely attached children were unable to use social pretend play for emotional mastery.

It appears that the less well-adjusted children did use social pretend play as a form of self-disclosure. Their play themes expressed their fears and unresolved conflict. However, as social pretend play by definition is dyadic and not individual activity, we wonder about the partners of these children. In the research, insecurely attached children were paired with other insecurely attached children and securely attached with securely attached partners. We suspect that some insecure-insecure pairs were dyads who shared similar fears and conflicts and were equally unable to imagine benign resolutions. In classroom situations these insecurely attached children might be avoided by more securely adjusted children who found their social pretend play themes too disturbing. Future research might manipulate the pairing of more and less-disturbed children. For example, an insecure-secure dyad might invent social pretend play that explored uncomfortable themes yet created more benign resolutions.

Future research might also examine the role of minor disturbances versus more serious and persistent problems in the use of social pretend play to achieve emotional mastery. For example, Fredrick's distress at the new baby may have been a minor disturbance in the life of a basically well-adjusted child. He was able to master his distress in the context of social pretend play within a well-established friendship group. What if Fredrick had been a newcomer to the peer group? Would the lack of friendships and social support from peers have made it impossible for the group to accommodate his social pretend play themes? Alternatively, is the theme of regression to baby sufficiently universal or sufficiently nonthreatening to be accommodated within any preschool peer group?

Paley (1988) suggests that some themes (e.g., suicide, as played out by a child refusing to evacuate an area of the block corner other children designated as "Lake Michigan ocean") are too perplexing or frightening to be easily incorporated into group play. Perhaps the children who are more seriously disturbed and/or have failed to integrate within the peer group generate pretend play themes that cannot become social pretend play themes. If a child's play themes frighten or threaten the others then although there is self-disclosure there is less likely to be intimacy and joint resolution. The child who generates such themes may be isolated or rejected by the group. See illustrative study #8.

Summary

In summary, we have suggested that once children become experts at negotiating and using social pretend play the function of play changes. Social pretend play is important both in helping children establish friendships and in providing opportunities for self-disclosure within friendships. Friends use social pretend play to express their fears and concerns and through these experiences develop trust and intimacy. We have suggested that interrelations between self-disclosure within pretend play and friendships are complex and in need of further research.

Three illustrative studies elaborate the themes of this review chapter. In "Friendship and Social Pretend Play: Illustrative Study #6," we compare the social pretend play of preschool children with long-term, contemporary, and no friendships. Given our interest in trust and intimacy, we were particularly concerned with the expression of these issues in the play of the children. This study illustrates the combination of naturalistic observation in the classroom to identify friendships with a quasi-laboratory procedure to assess social pretend play.

In the second illustrative study we expand our view of the child's social network to include parents and teachers as well as peer friendships' influences on children's social pretend play. Some of the children who participated in illustrative study #6 were also part of a longitudinal investigation exploring links among the parental and teacher attachment systems and the child's peer relationships. In "Multiple Attachments and Peer Relationships in Social Pretend Play," we examine the particular case of social pretend play quality. We ask whether adult attachment relationships are influential.

In our third and final illustrative study we expand the direction of the book to include an atypical population. In the review chapter we raised the question of whether the social pretend play of some children was too extreme in its exploration of emotional issues to permit joint play and resolution. To address this question we elicited and compared pretend play themes from abused and nonabused children.

10

Friendship and Social Pretend Play: Illustrative Study #6

Carollee Howes, Catherine Matheson, and Fang Wu

In the previous chapter we suggest that the function of social pretend play in preschool age children is to explore self-disclosure, intimacy, and trust. We further hypothesized that self-disclosure, intimacy, and trust would be specific to the social pretend play of friends, and less common in non-friend dyads. The purpose of this study is to examine these hypotheses by asking friends and nonfriends to use replica materials to construct a social pretend play script and then coding their play and social behaviors for self-disclosure, cohesiveness, and trust.

Friendships are reciprocated relationships with positive affective qualities. Each partner in a friendship must select the other. Researchers who examine early friendships report that the children engage in prosocial interactions and express positive affect in the context of interaction (Hinde et al. 1985; Howes 1983, 1988; Ross, Cheyne, & Lollis 1988). Most preschool children who have regular contacts with peers have at least one reciprocated friendship (Hinde et al. 1985; Howes 1983, 1988).

Two longitudinal studies have distinguished between long-term stable friendships and contemporary friendships. Howes (1983) found these two types of friendships to emerge during a yearlong study of a small preschool peer group. In this peer group long-term stable friends engaged in more complex social play than contemporary short-term friends. In a second longitudinal study, Howes (1988) found that ten percent of friendship dyads formed when children were toddler age remained stable over a three-year period and that sixty-five to seventy percent of the friendships formed when children were preschoolers remained stable over a two-year period. In this study, children who maintained a greater percent of their friends were rated as more socially competent. We suspect that long-term friendships provide a child with emotional and social support, and we would further expect this friendship to be characterized by trust, cohesiveness, and self-disclosure. Therefore, we expected long-term stable friendships to have higher levels of trust, cohesiveness, and self-disclosure than many contemporary friendships. Some contemporary friendships may be maintained and become long-term emotionally supportive relationships while others will fill different, more short-term functions.

In the current study we used two methods for identifying friendships: behavioral observations and sociometric techniques. Behavioral observations were used to identify long-term stable friendships. Sociometric techniques were used to identify contemporary friendships.

Behavioral observations to identify friendships assume that friends will behave differently than other pairs of children. There is support for this assumption especially in toddler and young preschool-age children. Friends, as compared to playmates, exchange more positive and less negative behaviors (Master & Furman 1981), show more reciprocity (Foot, Chapman, & Smith 1980; Lederberg et al. 1987), and are more responsive (Howes 1983). Furthermore, the behavior within friendship dyads of even toddler-age children differs from the behaviors that both partners give and receive in other social contexts (Ross & Lollis, in press). This last finding validates the use of observational methods to identify friendships as particular relationships rather than two sociable and friendly children who happen to play together.

In order to identify friendships with behavioral observations, the researcher must determine behavioral criteria. Several researchers have successfully used mutual preference and shared positive affect as criteria for identifying friendships (Hinde et al. 1985; Howes 1983, 1988; Vandell & Mueller 1980). The criterion of shared positive affect appears to best distinguish friendships (Howes 1983).

Identifying friendships by behavioral observation is most effective in younger children. As children reach the end of their preschool years they are more likely to play with nonfriend playmates as well as with friends (Howes 1983; Tessier & Boivin 1985). Fortunately, as children get older they become more reliable informants in sociometric interviews (Hymel 1983). Sociometric interviews in school-age children ask the children to nominate peers who are friends or who have particular behavioral attributes (Coie & Dodge 1983; Newcomb & Bukowski 1983; Perry 1979). Sociometric nominations are most frequently used to obtain social status classifications (e.g., Coie & Dodge 1983), but mutual nominations may also be used to identify friendships (Berndt et al. 1986; Howes 1988). Sociometric nominations in preschool children have been criticized for their relatively low reliability

(Hymel 1983). Recent work with children in child-care centers suggests that acceptable reliability on sociometric nominations may be obtained when children are cared for in well-established groups (Howes 1988).

An alternative sociometric assessment specifically designed for preschool children is a rating procedure using pictures of children's classmates (Asher et al. 1979). This procedure has acceptable test-retest reliability in preschool samples (Hymel 1983). Friendships have been successfully identified using a combination of the nomination and rating procedures (Berndt, Hawkins, & Hoyle 1986; Howes & Wu 1990). Children are considered friends if they nominate each other or if one child nominates the other and the partner gives the nominating child the highest rating.

There have been relatively few attempts to examine differential qualities of children's relationships. Two studies are particularly relevant to our purpose. Rosenberg (1983) examined social pretend play themes in children with varying maternal attachment histories. Her work is interesting in that it is an attempt to measure self-disclosure, cohesiveness, and trust within the social pretend play context. In the Rosenberg study, dyads with insecure attachment histories were unable to use social pretend play for emotional mastery; that is, they failed to resolve problems within play. However, they were able to explore disturbing social pretend play themes, presumably disclosing some of their fears and anxieties. Unfortunately, we know nothing of the relationships of the children in the dyads other than their attachment history. Park and Waters (1989) have more directly explored self-disclosure, trust, and cohesiveness in preschool-age children. They designed a Q-Set to measure relationship quality in preschool dyads, again with differing attachment histories. In the Park and Waters study, mothers selected the friend of the target child. Therefore, we do not know the history of the friendship. There have been no studies validating mother-nomination of friends with behavioral observations or sociometric techniques. Mothers may use different criteria for friendship identification than either friendship researchers or the children themselves. Although Park and Waters did not test our hypothesis that self-disclosure, cohesiveness, and trust are specific to the social pretend play of friends, and less common in nonfriend dyads, they provide an excellent tool for exploring these issues.

Our study is part of a larger study designed to examine the emergence of social competence and maladjustment with peers. In the larger study, seventy-two children have been followed from infancy into preschool. Thirteen of these children have remained in child care peer groups with a stable core group of children. Six of these children formed friendships as one-year-olds that they maintained into preschool. We used the children from the longitudinal study and their classmates to form twenty-four dyads of children, some long-term friendships, some contemporary friendships and some dyads of contemporary nonfriends. Long-term friendships were identified by behavioral observations and validated by sociometric techniques. Contemporary relationships were identified by sociometric nominations and ratings.

The contemporary nonfriends group included two different types of nonfriends—children who had friends but were not paired with them and children who did not have mutual friends within the classroom. We expected to see differences in the social pretend play of these two groups of children. Children who do not have friends may find it difficult to integrate their solitary pretend play with another child's play. In the group setting of the child-care center, a child without friends can avoid dyadic encounters more easily than in our experimental setting where we placed two children in a small room and instructed them to "make a story *together*."

Method

Subjects

Forty-eight children (seventeen girls) participated in this research. The children ranged in age from thirty-six to sixty months (mean age = forty-eight months). Sixty-four percent of the children were Euro-Americans 10 percent Afro-Americans, 20 percent Asian-American, and the remainder Middle Eastern. All of the children attended center-based child care full time. Thirteen (four girls) of the children were subjects in the longitudinal study. These children had been enrolled in child care prior to their first birthdays.

Procedures (*Sociometric*)

Nominations. We presented each child with an array of pictures of their classmates and asked them to hand the examiner the pictures of their three best friends.

Ratings. A modification of the Asher et al. (1979) sociometric measure was used to obtain sociometric ratings. The children were given pictures of their classmates, one by one, and asked to place them in a big, medium, or little bowl according to how much they wanted to play with that person. Children placed in the big bowl were given scores of 3 and those in the small bowl a score of 1.

Classification of contemporary friendships. We classified a dyad as *contemporary friends* if both children nominated the other or if one child nominated the other and the partner gave the nominating child a score of 3. Dyads were classified as *contemporary nonfriends* if neither child nominated the other and if neither child gave the other a score of 3. We divided contemporary nonfriends into two groups. The *nonfriends* group consisted of dyads in which neither partner had a contemporary friend. The *nonmutual friends* group consisted of dyads in which each partner had a contemporary friend but the children in the dyad were not contemporary friends.

Behavioral Observations

The thirteen longitudinal subjects were observed in their child-care settings at six-month intervals beginning in the first half of their second year (mean age of observation = seventeen months). At each observational interval we completed friendship scans. To be classified as a *long-term friend* the dyad had to appear in at least three friendship scans in each observational interval and had to be classified as a mutual contemporary friend. Interobserver reliability for identifying friends was kappa = .96.

The final sample consisted of four dyads of long-term friends, nine dyads of contemporary friends, eight dyads of nonmutual friends, and three dyads of nonfriends. The sex and ethnic composition of the friendship groups is presented in table 10.1.

Table 10.1 Sex and ethnic composition of dyads

	FRIENDS		NON-FRIENDS	
	Long term	Contemporary	Non-mutual	No Friends
<u>Number</u>	4	9	8	3
<u>Sex</u>				
Girl–girl	1	3	2	0
Boy–boy	2	4	4	3
Girl–boy	1	1	3	0
<u>Ethnicity</u>				
Same	3	5	8	0
Mixed	1	3	1	3

Social Pretend Play Session

Each dyad was videotaped as they played with replica toys representing trucks, boats, a motorcycle, a table, chairs, beds, and figures representing a family. The figures were appropriately sized to ride on the motorcycle, sit on the chairs, etc. A laminated map (2' x 4') was placed under the toys. The map contained an illustration of a pond, a road, and several ambiguous structures that could represent various parts of a village. The children were asked to make a story together with the toys. Each session lasted for twenty minutes. One adult remained in the room to film the session. She did not interact with the children. After fifteen minutes the children were told they only had three more minutes to play so they should finish making their story.

The entire videotape was used as the basis for completing the Park and Waters (1989) Q-Set for dyadic relationships. The first author who was blind to the dyad's friendship classification completed all of the Q-Sets. For the purposes of testing our hypotheses we selected Q-Set cluster scores representing self-disclosure and cohesiveness. We also included the one Q-Set item that directly rates whether the partners appear to trust each other. We also created a cluster of items to represent the coordinated and harmonious quality of the dyads's social pretend play (add items 2, 3, 54, and 45, and subtract items 19 and 22). Intercoder reliability for the cluster was established by double-coding five videotapes. Median intercoder reliability was kappa = .97 (range .87 to .99).

Results

The mean rating on each of the cluster scores for each friendship group are in table 10.2. Analysis of variance tests for linearity were used to test for trends from the no friends to the long-term friends groups. There were significant linear trends for self-disclosure, cohesiveness, and social pretend play. One-way analyses of variance and Scheffe post hoc tests were used to differentiate between groups. Long-term friends engaged in more self-disclosure than contemporary and nonmutual friends (Scheffe = .05). The no friends group engaged in less self-disclosure than all other groups (Scheffe = .05). Long-term friends were more cohesive than contemporary friends, contemporary friends more cohesive than nonmutual friends, and no friends less cohesive than nonmutual friends (Scheffe = .05). Long-term and contemporary friends engaged in more coordinated and harmonious social pretend play than nonmutual friends, nonmutual friends engaged in more social coordinated and harmonious pretend play than no friends (Scheffe = .05).

Table 10.2   Ratings of dyads with different degrees of friendship

	FRIENDS		NON-FRIENDS			
	Long-term	Contemporary	Non-mutual	No Friends	F for linearity	F for group
Ratings						
Self-disclosure						
	15.8	13.9	12.6	9.7	9.04**	3.14*
Cohesiveness						
	5.0	2.6	-1.2	-3.0	10.66**	3.63*
Trust						
	4.5	3.9	3.0	2.3	2.84	.95
Social Pretend						
	18.8	14.5	4.4	-4.0	19.33***	6.66**

Discussion

Our findings support our hypothesis that preschool friends are more likely to engage in self-disclosure within social pretend play than nonfriends. Moreover, the long-term friend dyads used more disclosure than contemporary friend dyads. In this case, self-disclosure was defined as telling or eliciting personal information. The level of self-disclosure was not particularly intimate (e.g., "When I go home my mommy going to take me bike riding"). This level of intimacy may be age-appropriate. Self-disclosure could have been defined in more subtle ways (e.g., fears expressed in the themes or scripts of the social pretend play). However, our limited knowledge of these children's lives precluded such an analysis. Future research may need to explore the forms of self-disclosure used by preschool-age children.

Friend dyads, particularly long-term friend dyads, were rated as more cohesive than nonfriend dyads. This supports our hypothesis that friends use social pretend play to explore intimacy. Surprisingly, there were no differences in ratings of trust. We suspect that a basic level of trust was fostered by enthusiastic support shown by the child-care teachers for the research project and by the particular child-care centers used. All of the children, even the nonfriend dyads, had been in small and stable peer groups for at least six months. Furthermore, the child-care centers used in the study explicitly teach group cooperation skills.

Friends, both long-term and contemporary, engaged in more coordinated and harmonious social pretend play than non-friends. While this finding was not unexpected given the previous research, it supports our notion that a significant function of social pretend play for preschool children is the exploration of intimate relationships.

11

Multiple Attachments and Peer Relationships in Social Pretend Play: Illustrative Study #7

Catherine Matheson

The theoretical and empirical literature on attachment supports the idea that children's relationships with significant caregiving adults have a strong impact on their social relationships with peers. This is particularly evident in the body of literature examining the relations between mother-child attachment quality and the development of social competence. Children with secure, as contrasted with insecure, attachment relationships with their mothers have been described as displaying and sharing more positive affect and engaging in increased amounts of pretend play (Waters, Wippman, & Sroufe, 1979), having higher self-esteem and increased levels of social competence (Sroufe 1983), and receiving more friendship nominations on sociometric measures (Easterbrook & Lamb 1979).

Of particular interest within the issue of attachment and peer relationships is a recent study by Park and Waters (1989). This study examined the relations between attachment patterns in best friend dyads of two- to five-year-old children and their ability to engage in competent social play in a laboratory setting. Dyads where both children had secure relationships with their mothers engaged in more harmonious and responsive play, and had a more positive conflict resolution style. Thus, a secure relationship with the mother was strongly associated with the ability to interact successfully with familiar peers.

The results of this study contribute significantly to the growing body of research on attachment and social development with peers. However, there are more issues in need of examination, specifically the type of social inter-action used to measure competence, and the influences of early friendship formation and multiple caregivers. Park and Waters (1989) looked at general social play rather than social pretend play, although representational toys were available to the children in their study. Competent social play is one marker of social competence, particularly during the first two years of child-hood (Howes 1988). Competent social pretend play may provide a more stringent test of the impact of attachment in the late toddler and preschool years (Howes 1988).

According to Howes, cooperative social pretend play involves not only the negotiation skills inherent in social play, but also the ability to communi-cate symbolic meaning and engage in role play. These skills, which emerge between three and five years of age, require flexibility and cooperation in order to be used successfully in pretend play. Therefore, the study of social pretend play may provide accurate evidence of higher levels of social compe-tence in the preschool period. Evidence from studies by Connolly and Doyle (1984) and Rosenberg (1983) support this conclusion. These two studies found relations between preschoolers' ability to participate in social pretend play and several measures of social competence such as sociometric status.

Howes (1988) and Corsaro (1981) have suggested that friendships may play an important role in the development of children's social play skills. Howes (1988) found that children with mutual friendships were able to enter play groups more easily, and engaged in more skillful interactions. Howes further noted that children who were unable to maintain friendships due to changes in child-care arrangements appeared less socially skilled than chil-dren who were able to stay with friends. These findings indicate that not only adult-child attachment, but also dyadic peer relationships, particularly long-term friendships, may be associated with social competence. There is a need to extend current work on the importance of peer friendships to include social pretend play as a measure of competent interaction between friends.

The final issue, concerning the impact of multiple caregivers and thus multiple attachment relationships, has gained importance over the past decade. Current concerns regarding multiple caregivers reflect a larger soci-etal concern with recent changes in the traditional family configuration, such as increases in maternal employment and nonmaternal child care. Children who enter some form of day care before their first birthdays form attachment relationships with at least two (and quite likely more) significant caregiving adults simultaneously. Through early multiple caregiver experiences, chil-dren construct the internal representations of relationships which are used to guide future social behavior. The current formulation of attachment theory is only beginning to describe the possible consequences of multiple attach-ments for the development of social relationships with peers.

Research on the impact of multiple caregivers to this point presents a complex picture. For example, Howes et al. (1988) found that children with secure attachments with both the mother and the day-care teacher were more socially competent in day care than children with mixed secure-insecure or two insecure attachment relationships. Main and Weston (1981) noted that a secure relationship with the father was associated with more friendliness with a stranger in the Strange Situation, particularly when the child had an insecure relationship with his mother. These studies suggest that one relationship may mediate the effects of another, or that different relationships may have different functions, particularly when the child is experiencing both secure and insecure attachment relationships.

Oppenheim, Sagi, and Lamb (1988), in studying children from an Israeli kibbutz, found that attachments to metapelet (group care provider) at one year predicted preschool social competence better than attachments to the mother or the father at one year. The measures of social competence, taken when the children were five years old, were done in an environment very similar to the early kibbutz setting. That is, the children interacted with their metapelet in a group context that closely paralleled the structure of the preschool. The authors suggested that attachment relationships with different caregivers may be associated with different aspects of development, particularly when caregivers perform different roles with respect to peer interactions.

The Oppenheim et al. study suggests a possible new perspective for examining the influences of multiple caregivers. The concept of the context within which relationships develop is introduced. If the child experiences relationships with several adults in different settings, the adults may have different behavior patterns and different expectations for child development, which would lead to distinct patterns of interaction. In addition, each setting would provide a unique set of opportunities for exploring the world of objects and peers. A child might experience more peer interaction within the context of day care, where she forms an attachment relationship to a day-care teacher. The day-care teacher has established rules and routines for appropriate behavior, and interacts with the child in ways that encourage desired behaviors. The child may use her relationship with the teacher as a guide in learning to play with peers, since the teacher is a much more salient figure in the day-care setting than her mother or father.

Findings from several other studies support the notion that context is important in determining the impact of multiple attachment relationships. Lamb et al. (1982) found that the child's sociability with a stranger was related to the attachment relationship with the father rather than the mother, with no indication of the mediating effects found by Main and Weston (1981). Lamb et al. concluded that there may not be one relationship serving as the prototype for all others, especially when a child has sufficient experiences with a variety of caregivers. Similar findings by Bridges, Connell, and Belsky (1988) led these researchers to conclude that different types of interaction patterns with the mother and father may indicate different roles for each in the child's development.

These findings suggest the intriguing possibility that multiple attachment relationships may have differential effects on the child's social development that may be at least partially related to the contexts in which the relationships occur. Although a fair amount of research has compared the impact of quality of attachments to the mother and father, much less has been done in the area of parent and day-care teacher attachment relationships. Due to the increasing numbers of young children entering day care before their first birthdays, there is a need to investigate the impact of multiple attachments on social development when at least one adult-child relationship is nonfamilial.

The purpose of this study is to examine the relations between mother-child and day-care teacher-child attachments and the functioning of different types of peer relationships within social pretend play. The previous study (Chapter 10) found that the level of friendship within a given pair of children was associated with the degree of cooperation and intimacy achieved in social pretend play. The current study investigates this association from the perspective of each child's attachment history. We expect that the quality of relationships with both the mother and day-care teacher will be associated with the level of friendship and degree of cooperation and intimacy. Children with secure attachment histories are more likely to have stable, long-term friendships and use social pretend play to resolve social conflicts and explore self-disclosure.

However, we expect the results to become more complicated when children have nonconcordant attachment histories with the mother and day-care teacher. We have information in the current study on the children's attachment security to the mother and teacher at two time points (ages one and four years). The friendship and social pretend play measures were taken at four years of age. Although all children in the study had secure relationships with their mothers at age one, there were shifts in attachment quality for both caregivers from time one to time two, and there were nonconcordant attachments with the mother and teacher at each time point.

Traditional attachment theory suggests that attachment quality at time one (infancy) would be more strongly associated with long-term friendships and successful social interaction in preschool. Attachment theorists such as Lamb et al. (1985) argue that the nature of concurrent relationships (time two) would be more important. Sroufe (1983) stresses the importance of continuity in relationships, which would suggest that those children with secure relationships at both times would be the most competent. Therefore, we were particularly interested in the social pretend play of those children with shifts in attachment quality.

The children in the present study are part of a larger, longitudinal study on children's attachment relationships and their social competence within the day-care setting. All the children in the longitudinal study entered day care in infancy. Of this larger group, twenty-three children have maintained at least one stable peer contact through preschool. These twenty-three children have experienced several changes of caregivers as they moved from the infant to toddler to preschool classes. Thus, quality of attachment was assessed with different teachers at time one and two. However, the quality of each classroom, as assessed with the Early Childhood Environment Rating Scale (Harms & Clifford 1980), was highly similar, with total ratings ranging from 3.0 to 4.0, indicating each classroom met, but did not exceed, basic requirements for good quality care. Therefore, we suggest that the contexts for all teacher attachments within this sample are comparable, and we have treated teacher-child attachment as a measure of a context separate from mother-child attachment.

Method

Subjects

Twenty-three children (eight girls) participated in this research. The children ranged in age from thirteen to eighteen months at time one, and thirty-eight to fifty-three months at time two. Sixty-four percent of the children were Euro-Americans, 10 percent Afro-American, 20 percent Asian-American and the remainder Middle Eastern. All of the children attended center-based child care full-time, and were enrolled prior to their first birthdays.

Procedures

Attachment ratings. As part of the larger longitudinal study, the children were observed in their day-care centers at times one and two. At each time point, two observers collected information about the child's interaction with her primary day-care teacher and interactions during reunion with and separation from her mother. Each child was observed for an average of three-and-one-half hours by each observer over a two-week period at time one, and again at time two.

Each observer then completed the Waters and Deane Attachment Q-Sort (1985) for both teacher-child and mother-child relationships. Separate

Q-Sorts were completed at times one and two. Results of the two Q-Sorts for each relationship were averaged, then correlated with the criterion sorts for security provided by Waters and Deane (1985).

Friendship Selection

During the behavioral observations described in the preceding section, friendship scans were also completed on each child in the study. Children were observed for twelve one-minute intervals during the course of each hour of observation. During each one-minute interval, the presence or absence of a friendship interaction was noted for each child. Three criteria had to be met in order to record a friendship: mutual preference, mutual positive affect, and the ability to sustain action role reversal play.

These scans were used to determine the existence of long term friendships for the children in the study. To be classified as having a long-term friend, a child had to appear in at least three friendship scans with the same partner at time one, and again at time two. At time two, nine children were classified as having long-term friends.

Social Pretend Play Session

The nine children classified as having long-term friends were paired with those friends, and the other fourteen children were paired with acquaintances from the same class. The resulting dyads were videotaped in 20-minute pretend play sessions in a separate room at the day-care center. Small replica toys representing trucks, boats, a motorcycle, tables, chairs, beds, and family figures were available for play. The toys were placed on a table covered by a laminated map (2' x 4') with illustrations of a road, pond, bridge, and three buildings that could represent various parts of a town.

One adult stayed in the room with the children to operate the video camera. The adult asked the children to make a story together using the toys, and warned the children when they had three more minutes to play. Otherwise, the adult did not interact with the children.

Each 20-minute video session was used to complete the Park and Waters Dyadic Relationships Q-Set (Park & Waters 1989). Researchers who were blind to the children's attachment and friendship classifications completed the Q-Sets. Individual item scores were added to create eight cluster scores. Seven of these clusters came from the Park and Waters study, and consisted of Coordinated Play, Harmony, Positive Social Orientation, Cohesiveness, Control, Self-Disclosure, and Responsiveness. An additional cluster was created to represent coordinated and harmonious social pretend play (adding scores for items 2, 3, 54, and 45, and subtracting scores for items 19 and 22). For the purposes of this study, mean Q-Set cluster scores were used as measures of individual abilities within dyadic pretend play.

Results

All the children in this study were classified as having a secure attachment relationship with their mothers at time one. Therefore, only attachment classifications with teachers were used in data analysis of time one. A two-way ANOVA was performed on the eight Q-Set cluster scores with existence of long-term friendship and attachment classification with the teacher at time one as the independent variables. See table 11.1. There was a significant friendship-by-attachment classification interaction for aggressive control of partner ($F(1,22) = 5.9, p < .05$). Significant main effects for friendship were found for aggressive control of partner ($F(1,22) = 4.5, p < .05$), positive social orientation ($F(1,22) = 5.2, p < .05$), coordinated play ($F(1,22) = 4.3, p < .05$), and complexity of fantasy play ($F(1,22) = 7.6, p < .05$).

By time two, several children had experienced shifts in attachment quality with their mother as well as with the caregiver. Therefore, relations between Q-Set cluster scores, friendship status, and attachment security with the mother and caregiver during preschool were examined using two-way ANOVAs. There were no significant interaction effects for either analysis, nor were any main effects found for attachment classification with the mother or teacher at time two. The main effects for friendship status were the same as those listed in table 11.1.

In order to examine the social pretend play behaviors of children with nonconcordant attachment qualities, children were grouped according to both attachment classifications at time two, and their Q-Set cluster scores were compared using a one-way ANOVA procedure (see table 11.2). Significant differences were found between groups on self-disclosure ($F(1,22) = 7.3, p < .01$) and coordinated play ($F(1,22) = 3.5, p < .05$). For both clusters, children with one secure relationship were significantly different from children with no or two secure relationships (LSD test, $p < .05$).

Chi-square tables were used to examine the relations between shifts in attachment security from time one to two and the children's friendship classifications. The numbers and types of shifts in security are described in table 11.3. Table 11.4 illustrates the single significant finding of this analysis. Children who moved from insecure with the caregiver at time one to secure with the caregiver at time two all had long-term friends. Children who remained insecure with the caregiver had no long-term friends (Fisher exact test, $p = .05$).

Table 11.1 Means, S.D.s, and F-Tests on Q-Set Clusters for Friendship Status and Attachment Classification with Day-Care Teacher at Time One

Q-SET CLUSTERS	NO LONG-TERM FRIEND			LONG-TERM FRIEND			F-TESTS	
	insecure	secure	total	insecure	secure	total	friendship	attachment by friendship
positive social orientation	21.0 (6.9)	18.1 (5.8)	18.7 (5.9)	27.7 (8.9)	24.6 (1.1)	26.3 (6.6)	5.2*	.00
cohesiveness	4.0 (2.0)	2.9 (4.3)	3.1 (3.9)	5.2 (1.3)	5.8 (1.5)	5.5 (1.3)	2.2	.28
harmonious play	1.0 (8.5)	-2.4 (6.4)	-1.6 (6.8)	4.5 (12.1)	4.7 (1.5)	4.6 (8.6)	2.5	.23
control	20.3 (4.0)	31.0 (6.2)	28.7 (7.3)	22.7 (5.3)	20.4 (5.4)	21.7 (5.2)	4.5*	5.9*
self-disclosure	15.3 (3.5)	11.5 (2.7)	12.4 (3.2)	14.1 (3.5)	15.6 (4.3)	14.8 (3.7)	1.8	3.0
coordinated play	3.7 (9.3)	-6.2 (10.6)	-4.1 (10.8)	9.6 (4.0)	4.8 (10.8	7.5 (7.7)	4.3*	.32
responsive	20.3 (6.4)	14.7 (5.3)	15.9 (5.8)	21.7 (6.9)	19.1 (2.1)	20.6 (5.3)	1.7	.35
fantasy play	12.7 (5.5)	3.5 (8.3)	5.4 (8.5)	17.3 (2.7)	15.1 (7.6)	16.3 (5.1)	7.6*	1.1

* $p < .05$

Table 11.2 Means, S.D.s, and F-Tests for Q-Set Clusters for Concordant and Nonconcordant Attachment Classifications in Preschool

Q-SET CLUSTERS	INSECURE M INSECURE T	INSECURE M SECURE T	SECURE M INSECURE T	SECURE M SECURE T	F
positive social orientation	19.5 (2.1)	24.8 (4.2)	23.7 (6.1)	20.2 (9.2)	.54
cohesiveness	2.5 (3.6)	3.8 (1.9)	5.0 (1.0)	3.4 (4.2)	.25
harmonious play	-1.5 (14.8)	3.2 (5.3)	4.7 (5.0)	-1.3 (9.8)	.54
control	26.5 (10.6)	23.8 (6.4)	17.3 (1.2)	29.2 (6.8)	2.7
self-disclosure	10.5 (2.1)	16.0 (4.2)	17.7 (2.3)	11.3 (1.6)	7.3**
coordinated play	-11.5 (3.5)	8.4 (7.3)	9.0 (7.0)	-3.2 (11.2)	3.5*
responsive	13.0 (4.2)	20.6 (4.8)	22.7 (2.5)	15.9 (6.7)	2.0
fantasy play	0.0 (2.8)	14.6 (8.8)	15.0 (7.0)	6.9 (9.4)	2.1

M = mother
T = teacher
* $p < .05$
** $p < .01$

Table 11.3 Shifts in Attachment Classification

CLASSIFICATION		NUMBER OF CHILDREN	
Time One	Time Two	Mother	Teacher
Secure	Secure	14	11
Insecure	Secure	0	5
Secure	Insecure	7	3
Insecure	Insecure	0	2

Table 11.4 Shifts in Attachment Quality with Teacher and Friendship Status at Time Two

| Classification | | NUMBERS OF CHILDREN WITH: | |
		No Long-Term Friend	Long-Term Friend
Time One	Time Two		
Insecure	Secure	0	5
Insecure	Insecure	2	0

Discussion

The results of this study must be considered as preliminary findings, due to the small sample size. Both children's attachment relationships with their mother and teacher and their friendships appear to be associated with the degree of competence achieved in social pretend play during the preschool period, but in rather complicated ways.

All the children in this study had secure attachment relationships with their mothers at time one, as represented by correlations with the security criterion sort of the Waters and Deane Attachment Q-Set (1985). There were some shifts in attachment by time two, but contemporaneous preschool attachment relationships with the mother alone were not directly related to pretend play behavior with peers. However, when relationships with teachers were also considered, attachment quality became a factor in peer behavior. Children with a secure relationship with either their mother or teacher at time two showed higher levels of intimacy and coordination of play with peers than children with no secure relationships or two secure relationships.

This finding is counterintuitive to a general reading of attachment theory, where a child with two secure relationships should be at least as socially competent as a child with one secure relationship. The limitations of the current study prevent any definite conclusions from being drawn. However, research on children's social orientation to peers and adults in day care (Galluzzo et al. 1988) provides a possible direction for further inquiry. This research suggests that children who are almost exclusively adult-oriented in day care are less socially competent than children who are equally interested in adults and peers. Perhaps many of the children with two secure attachment relationships in the current study were more adult-oriented by preschool, thus spending less time with peers and having fewer opportunities to develop high levels of intimacy and responsiveness in pretend play. It may be necessary in future research to combine measures of attachment and social orientation in order to understand the relative impact of adult and peer relationships on social competence.

The results of the current study do indicate that, at least by preschool age, one secure attachment relationship may be all that is necessary for competent functioning in dyadic social pretend play. These results also point to the fact that the secure relationship does not necessarily have to be with the mother, although there was a very slight trend for children secure with their mother to have more competent scores.

However, the attachment system did not appear to be the sole mediator of successful functioning with peers. Early, stable friendship formation was also implicated in preschool social pretend play skills. Children who were both secure with their teacher at time one and had a long-term friendship beginning at time one were less likely to attempt aggressive control techniques. Children with long-term friends were more likely to help and like their partners, respond to their partners' actions and play themes, and engage in more complex fantasy play as preschoolers. The lack of significant main effects for contemporaneous adult attachment relationships in preschool seems to suggest that peer relationships may become more critical than adult relationships in the development of social competence once children advance beyond the toddler stage.

Further evidence for the importance of the peer system in social development comes from examining the shifts in security of attachment to teacher between time one and time two. All of the children who moved from an insecure to a secure relationship with their teachers had a long-term friend. These children were observed in friendship interactions at time one, while they still had less than optimal relationships with their teachers. While it is true that all of these children did begin day care with secure relationships with their mothers, there was a larger group who also had an early secure attachment to their mother and did not establish early friendships. Therefore, caution is necessary in describing the impact of attachment relationships for this group of children.

Due to the exploratory nature of this study, no definite conclusions can be drawn. However, the results raise questions concerning the relative contributions of adult and peer relationships to social development when stable, long-term peer relationships are available in the day-care setting. Perhaps children who were able to form early, close peer relationships used these relationships as mediators between themselves and their teachers. One possible hypothesis would be that stable long-term friendships serve as a buffer for children with insecure or changing adult relationships, and allow the children to explore and improve their relationships with adults from a secure base with their peers.

The findings of this study indicate that both early and concurrent adult-child relationships, as well as early peer interactions, may be significant factors in the development of social competence. A complex picture begins to emerge, where relationships with the mother and teacher assume rather undifferentiated but necessary roles and friendships with peers become important as mediators of social competence and teacher-child relationships, particularly as children move toward preschool and increased independence.

12

Self-disclosure in the Pretend Play of Physically and Sexually Abused Children: Illustrative Study #8

Nan Tarlow and Carollee Howes

We have argued throughout this book that the themes and scripts of social pretend play represent a form of self-disclosure for preschool-age children. This is not a new argument: Freud and Piaget and many teachers and therapists suggest that children's fantasy play represents attempts to make sense of their experiences and that children use their play to recreate and make more manageable scary or unintelligible situations. The other illustrative studies in this book have focused on the ability of children to use self-disclosure within social pretend play. In social pretend play children have to accommodate their own fantasy themes with those of a partner in order to produce mutually satisfying social pretend play. In contrast, this chapter will focus on individual pretend play.

We used a doll play research strategy to compare the fantasy play of children known to have been physically or sexually abused with the fantasy play of similar-age children with no known history of abuse. Doll play as a research strategy has a checkered history. It was particularly popular in the 1940s and 1950s. Many research studies used doll play instead of observations or interviews to assess children's behavior and development (see Levin & Wardwell 1962). For example, Levin and Sears (1956) used doll play to assess children's aggressive behaviors and found children who were more aggressive in the doll play to also be the children whose mothers reported excessive aggressive behaviors. A series of studies under R. Sears at the Iowa Child Welfare Station varied the degree of structure introduced by the experimenter in order to produce more meaningful, less exploratory play (Levin & Wardwell 1962). It was concluded that when the doll play materials are structured by the experimenter and when the materials are accurate replicas of people and furniture the children are most likely to generate meaningful stories. Despite efforts to standardize doll play procedures, there was ambiguity about the material produced by the children. For example, was it a replication of the child's real life or was it wishes and fantasy? Doll play fell out of favor as a research strategy. It was replaced with more "objective" measures.

Recently several investigators (e.g., Oppenheim 1987, 1989; Bretherton, Ridgeway, & Cassidy, in press) have begun to use doll play techniques as a way of assessing the child's representation of relationships. This new doll play research is rooted in attachment theory. According to Bowlby (1973), children represent their experiences within relationships with significant caregivers in internal working models. Children who experience rejection and insensitivity are expected to have working models that describe caregivers as unavailable or inconsistent. Doll interviews assess children's internal models by asking them to enact separation experiences. Children whose doll play stories reflect secure relationships with caregivers are assessed with independent measures as being securely attached (Bretherton et al. in press; Oppenheim 1989). Thus, it appears that the stories created by the child during structured doll play interviews tap into the child's internal working model of relationships. In other words, they are a form of self-disclosure.

A large body of research suggests that in the general population approximately 60 to 70 percent of children are securely attached to their mothers (Ainsworth et al. 1978). Not surprisingly, most of the separation stories produced by children in the Bretherton and Oppenheim studies were harmonious. For example, children acted out stories in which parents told grandparents to look after children, fathers hugged their children when they returned from trips, and mothers cleaned up spilled juice without hitting the child.

We expected that the stories produced by abused children in our study would be more conflictual. Children who have been abused are less likely than nonmaltreated children to have internal working models representing consistent and sensitive caregiving. There are no prior studies of elicited doll play in abused children. Reidy (1977) used a directed play situation and reported that six-year-old physically abused children engage in more aggressive play than non-maltreated children. Observational studies of behavior with peers can provide indirect evidence of children's internal working models of the self and other. There are a number of observational studies of physically abused children playing with peers that report heightened frequencies of aggressive behaviors (George & Main 1979; Hoffman-Plotkin & Twentyman 1984; Howes & Eldredge 1985). Studies of sexually abused children are less numerous and less consistent. Some observers reported less aggressive behaviors than control samples (Shaw & Meier 1983); others elevated levels of aggression (Conte & Dodge 1983).

Method

Sample

Forty children between the ages of forty-eight and seventy-six months (mean age 63.4 months) participated in this study. Sixteen of the children had been sexually abused, eight had been physically abused, and sixteen had no known history of sexual abuse, physical abuse, or neglect, and were not currently in treatment for any behavior problem. All of the children in the two abused groups had been identified as abused and referred for treatment by either the court, the Department of Public Social Services, the parents, or a mental health professional. Any child with a history of reported or suspected neglect was excluded from the study, as was any child known to have suffered both physical and sexual abuse. Children with any known developmental disability, and children with any severe emotional disturbance such as autism or schizophrenia, were also excluded from the study.

All of the children were from low-income families. Their average monthly income in 1985 was $1176.40 and there were no differences between the incomes of the families of the sexually abused, physically abused, and nonabused children. Half of the children in the nonabused group came from single-parent families and half lived in two-parent families. Three of the sexually abused children and three of the physically abused children lived in foster or group homes, one of the children in each of these groups lived with their grandparents. The remainder of the abused children lived in single-parent (38 percent each of sexually and physically abused children) or two-parent families (one physically abused child and six sexually abused).

More girls than boys (63 percent) were in the sexually abused group while more boys (63 percent) were in the physically abused group. This unequal distribution mirrors the distribution of sexually and physically abused children in the population. The nonabused group was equally divided between girls and boys. The two abused groups were primarily Euro-American (63 percent in both groups) and Mexican-American (31 percent of sexually abused and 38 percent of physically abused) in ethnicity. The nonabused group was 81 percent Mexican-American and 19 percent Euro-American.

Procedure

Each child played individually with a clinically trained adult. When the child entered the testing room a family of dolls (adult male and female, female and male child dolls) and appropriate-sized furniture were set up on a table. The family was seated on chairs at a table and the nonsexed baby doll was placed as if crawling on the floor, next to the table. The child was asked to play with the dolls ("Make the dolls do whatever you like") for five minutes. Following the free-play period the adult introduced fifteen different vignettes to the child. In each vignette the dolls, furniture, and opening statements were standardized. The child was asked to complete the story. A new vignette was not introduced until the child indicated that he or she had finished the story. Throughout the session the adult refused to make play suggestions but remained supportive of the child.

The vignettes were designed to represent situations that are routine aspects of family life (e.g., the parent dolls leave the child with a baby-sitter, or the mother doll won't let the child have a cookie before dinner). Seven vignettes were designed to elicit aggressive play, four to elicit sexual play, and four were neutral. A list of vignettes is presented in table 12.1. All vignettes except a family going to their favorite place were counterbalanced. This was always presented last in order to end the session with a positive experience. Sessions lasted for between 20 and 45 minutes. All sessions were videotaped.

Measures

Each vignette was coded for the following measures: *Ability to sustain play:* The child remained in the room playing with the dolls. Sustained play was not scored if the child left the doll play to find parent, go to the bathroom, etc., or was distracted by other things in the room and unable to attend to the doll play or was extremely restless and fidgeting; *Aggressive Play responses:* The child had the dolls hit, spank, push, bite, yell, demand, or sarcastically belittle another, and/or the story included serious injury ("his face was smashed"), hospitalization, or death. A rater blind to the identity of the subjects coded the videotapes. Twenty-five percent of the videotapes were double-coded for reliability purposes. Interrater reliability was 95 percent agreement.

Results

Differences in Ability to Sustain Play

Children who had been physically abused were less able to sustain play than the sexually abused and the nonabused children (5 point scale in which 5 equals unable to sustain play; x̄ (physically abused) = 4.5; x̄ (sexually abused) = 3.8; x̄ (control) = 3.0; F(2,37) = 6.79, $p < .01$, least significant differences post hoc test = .05). Sexually abused children and physically abused children were similar in ability to sustain play.

Table 12.1 Vignettes Used to Elicit Doll Play

SITUATIONS DESIGNED TO SUGGEST AN AGGRESSIVE PLAY RESPONSE

A friend wants S's favorite toy. What does S do?

S's little brother bites S. What does S do?

S's friends won't let him/her play with them. What does S do?

S's friend tells on S. What does S do?

S's friend punches S. What does S do?

S's mom won't let S have a cookie before dinner. What does S do?

Mom is yelling at S. Why? What does S do?

SITUATIONS DESIGNED TO SUGGEST A SEXUAL PLAY RESPONSE

Who does S tell when she/he has to go "potty"? What happens?

S is tired. Who puts S down for a nap? What happens?

Parent(s) go out and leave S with a baby-sitter. What do they do together?

NEUTRAL SITUATIONS

The free play period.

A friend is visiting the S doll. What do they do?

S is crying. What happened?

S had a scary dream, a nightmare. What was it about? Who was in it?

Family is going to their favorite place. What is it like? Where is it? Who goes? What happens?

S refers to "subject" doll, that is, a child doll the same sex as the particular subject.

Differences in Aggressive Play Responses

Sexually abused children enacted more aggressive play responses than either physically abused or nonabused children (Episodes with aggression: x (Sexually abused) = 4.3; x̄ (physically abused = 3.5; x̄ (control) = 1.7 F(2,37) = 4.86, $p < .01$, least significant differences post hoc test = .05). Physically abused and nonabused children were similar in aggressive play responses.

Play Vignettes That Differentiated Between
Children of Different Histories of Abuse

Some vignettes were more successful than others in eliciting play that distinguished between children with different histories of abuse. While these are low-frequency behaviors, impossible to meaningfully analyze in a statistical sense, these qualitative differences are suggestive of future research directions. In general, vignettes involving the entire family of dolls rather than the child doll and a friend produced the most variance in response. Both the initial free play situation—the family sitting at the table and the instruction to play any way that you would like—and the last situation, the family going to their favorite place, elicited aggression from the physically abused children. The final situation also elicited sexual play from the sexually abused children. Similarly, when the mother doll yelled at the child doll all groups of children reacted with aggression. The child doll was scolded and/or spanked. However, only the physically abused children were unable to sustain the play in this vignette. They were distracted, or asked to leave the room.

Discussion

The findings of this study suggest that pretend play can serve as a form of self-disclosure. Children with different caregiving histories produced very different responses in an elicited doll play situation. Children who had been physically abused found the doll play interview disturbing. They were distracted and had trouble finishing the play. Sexually abused children engaged in more physical aggression than the other children. This is in contrast to the Bretherton et al. (in press) and Oppenheim (1987, 1989) normative samples of preschoolers who expressed little conflict.

This study is limited by very small sample sizes, particularly in the physically abused groups. It was difficult to identify "pure" cases of abuse. Many children identified as physically abused had also been sexually abused or neglected and therefore were not included in the study. Even with this limitation the results suggest that engaging children in structured or elicited doll play may be a useful diagnostic as well as research tool.

13

Conclusions

We have suggested that the function of social pretend play changes as children become more adept at managing the complexity of the play. Initially, the function of the play is to master the communication of meaning. Once children are able to play pretend with a partner, the content of the play becomes more important and leads to the development of play negotiation skills. Issues of autonomy, control, and compromise underlie the negotiation of social pretend play. The function of pretend play becomes exploring these issues, and once these issues are resolved within social pretend play, the function of the play changes again. Social pretend play becomes an opportunity to explore issues of intimacy and trust.

The remainder of this chapter will summarize and integrate the results of the illustrative studies with the theory chapters.

Mastery of the Communication of Meaning

We have argued that the first function of social pretend play is the mastery of the communication of meaning. We suggest that developmental changes in cognitive and linguistic abilities contribute to a child's growing social pretend play skills. Future research may help us understand these convergent developments. Do cognitive and linguistic or communicative capacities initially limit and then permit children's more sophisticated social pretend play? Some of the evidence presented in Chapter 2 leads to this conclusion. Alternatively, from a Vygotskian point of view, all cognitive development occurs within a social context. Thus, developmental change occurs not because the cognitive child permits a change but because the child experiences more complex play in the context of social interaction. Thus, the child's attempts to engage in social pretend play with a partner facilitate the mastery of the communication of meaning. The two illustrative studies pursue this point.

Beizer and Howes in illustrative study #1 explored mother-toddler social pretend play. Toddlers engaged in more elaborate symbolic pretend play with their mothers than when playing alone. However, the findings do not point to a clear notion of the direction of effects. Were mothers generally responsible for structuring their children's pretend activity or did children initiate activities that the mothers then joined or followed? Beizer and Howes suggest that in order to address this question future research should explore the mother's systems of organizing children's play.

Howes and Unger in illustrative study #2 examined strategies used by same-age toddlers to construct social pretend play. This illustrative study differs from the previous one in that there is no skilled play partner to either shape or extend the toddlers' social pretend play attempts. However, the results of this study indicated that in the absence of an experienced and knowledgeable social partner toddlers use strategies that are functionally similar to those used by more skilled partners. Successful social pretend occurred when the toddlers used strategies that required a response and/or were dependent on the pretend action of the partner. It seems as if same-age toddler social pretend play works when the individual strategies of the partners provide a framework for the play. Social pretend play can be thought of as an externalization of internal symbolic processes. Through their struggles to communicate in play the meaning of their symbols, children initiate social pretend play with a partner. Play can only continue if the partner can understand the meaning and accommodate his or her own symbols within the play. Illustrative study #3, Farver's study of Mexican and American children, suggests that these attempts to communicate meaning are not limited to industrialized or economically advanced countries. In both the Mexican and American contexts children negotiated social pretend play, though Mexican children were less likely than American children to provide narrative story lines for their play. In both cultures children constructed shared meanings during the course of their play by building on their partner's ideas and actions as the play unfolded. The illustrative studies from this period suggest that in successful social pretend play partners provide an organization for the play and that this organization facilitates and extends the play.

Understanding the mastery of the communication of meaning function of social pretend play requires the examining of relations between the strategies used by each partner and the resulting social pretend play. Existing studies point to transition points in this process, age periods when the type of strategies and the type of play undergo organizational shifts. These transition points deserve further investigation.

Further investigation is also needed to understand the role of linguistic or communicative competence in the mastery of the communication of meaning in social pretend play. Few studies have independently assessed communicative competence and social pretend play yet it appears obvious that children who have difficulty communicating will be less able to engage in social pretend play. Finally, while there is a growing body of research examining the roles of various types of partners in social pretend play, there are few studies relating qualitative aspects of the partner's relationships to success in mastering the communication of meaning in social pretend play. In order to communicate meaning and to play social pretend play, the partners must want to pursue the often difficult task of coordinating and accommodating symbols. We suspect that the motivation to engage in social pretend play comes in part from the enjoyment of mastery and in part from the trust in the other that makes safe and enjoyable play possible.

Exploring Issues of Control and Compromise by Negotiating Social Pretend Play

The descriptive literature on social pretend play is clear that once children understand that they can share or communicate meaning in social pretend play they proceed to seemingly endless negotiations of which meanings in which form and which order will be played. We have related these play negotiations to more general developmental themes of autonomy, control, and compromise.

In reviewing the literature on the negotiation function of social pretend play, we speculate that the child's relationships with others, particularly with parents and friends, may influence individual differences in a child's ability to master this function of play. The two illustrative studies in this section elaborate this point. Olivia Unger in illustrative study #4 reports some preliminary findings from a study of maternal beliefs about mediating social pretend play and children's peer networks. The first striking finding from her work is that within a very small sample of what initially appeared to be a very homogeneous group of well-educated and affluent mothers there are extremely diverse notions of what is appropriate for children's play with peers. These beliefs appear to develop as a function of the mothers' interactions with their children in a variety of peer contexts. Maternal beliefs about appropriate behavior with peers appeared rooted in the particular experiences they had had as managers of peer contacts rather than drawn simply from the general value system of the mother. We need further research to examine the relation between maternal beliefs and children's social pretend play.

Howes and Rodning in illustrative study #5 directly examine relations between individual differences in social pretend play negotiations with peers and children's relationships with others. The relationship with another in this case is the child's attachment to the mother as measured in infancy. Howes and Rodning report that children with an insecure attachment history found it difficult to engage in social pretend play at all, that their social pretend play was likely to be interrupted by conflict, and once a conflict arose these children could not repair and continue the play. These findings suggest that children with insecure attachment histories may lack the flexibility to successfully negotiate social pretend play. Future research needs to examine what goes wrong in the process of social pretend play negotiation.

Our review of the social pretend play negotiation literature suggests that we have a good understanding of the processes involved. The relations between social pretend play negotiations and other developmental phenomena are less well understood. Social pretend play negotiation could be characterized as a form of social problem solving yet there has been little attempt to tie together negotiations with the literature on the development of social cognition. Likewise, pretend negotiations appear to be related to issues of autonomy and control and there have been few attempts to link mother-child social pretend negotiations to the larger literature on compliance and socialization. We also encourage research pursuing relations between the child's relations with adults, child-care teachers as well as mothers and fathers, and with same-age friends and the child's flexibility in social pretend play negotiations. We hope that our review and illustrative studies will stimulate these research efforts.

Issues of Intimacy and Trust Within Social Pretend Play

In our review we suggest that once children have mastered the communication of meaning and negotiation functions of social pretend play they are able to use social pretend play to explore intimacy and trust. At this point in our model we have achieved concordance with Gottman and colleagues who suggest that social pretend play has a central role in the development of social relationships and social competence because it allows children to experiment with trust and intimacy through self-disclosure.

Our illustrative studies are first and primitive attempts to untangle relations between self-disclosure in social pretend play and the child's intimate relationships with others, adults and peers. Howes, Matheson, and Wu in illustrative study #6 compared qualitative aspects of the social pretend play of four groups of preschoolers—children who had maintained long-term friendships over several years, children who were currently friends, children who had friends but were not paired with them, and children who did not have friends. Children who were friends were most likely to use self-disclosure in their play and long-term friends were more likely than contemporary friends to self-disclose. These findings support our notion that the function of social pretend play between friends in the preschool year is to explore issues of intimacy and trust. It suggests that the same children who were able to sustain a friendship over a long period are best able to self-disclose in play. The security of the friendship may have enhanced the play or the children who were particularly harmonious from an early age may have been able to sustain the friendship.

Catherine Matheson in illustrative study #7 begins the process of untangling antecedents to self-disclosure between friends in social pretend play by examining relationship histories in a small subsample of the children studied in chapter 10. These children's relationships with their mothers and child-care teachers had been assessed and categorized as one-year-olds. A complex picture emerges from this matrix of relationships. Children rated as more sociable with their mothers as infants were more competent social pretend players as preschoolers. Children who were initially rated as insecure with their teachers as infants and who formed a long term friendship during that period were rated in preschool both as secure with teachers and as competent in social pretend play. Children who were rated as insecure with teachers as infants and who did not form a long-term friendship were rated as preschoolers as insecure with teachers and less competent in pretend play. These findings, based on a very small sample and requiring replication, raise interesting questions about the independence and interdependence of relationships with adults and peers.

Our final illustrative study, Tarlow and Howes's illustrative study #8, begins the process of moving our discussion of social pretend play as a means for self-disclosure toward issues of prevention and intervention. Even in a fairly structured play situation children with different caregiving histories engaged in dissimilar pretend play. The paradigm used in this study could be easily modified to examine social pretend play in dyads of children with different histories of caregiving or different histories of relationships. We wonder if such experiences might help children who have trouble spontaneously using social pretend play as a means to achieve trust and intimacy.

While the research to date is clear that social pretend play, friendship, and self-disclosure are linked, we are less clear about how. Children who are already friends may use social pretend play to self-disclose. Children may use self-disclosure to become friends. Children who were friends may find the nature of the self-disclosure within social pretend play too emotionally laden or simply not interesting and therefore end or "cool down" their friendship. Research in this area is difficult because of the limitations of our available methodology and of the children's capacity for self-reflective talk. Although we are now able to videotape "private" social pretend play we are not always certain of how to code intimacy and trust. For example, we find it relatively easy to judge connectedness to others when two girls tenderly cooperate in putting the babies to bed and very difficult to judge connectiveness to others when two boys spend fifteen minutes in harmonious and violent motorcycle racing. We have not yet discovered how to ask these five-year-old motorcycle racers to explain how or if the play deepens their friendships.

Summary

In summary, we have suggested both a developmental model for changes in the function of social pretend play and its links to more general social competence. We encourage further research to test and expand this model. The second theme in this book is the issue of individual differences. We have pointed out issues that appear to us to be fruitful beginnings in attempting to understand the influences of children's developmental characteristics, partner characteristics, and relationships between children and others on their development of social pretend play. We hope that our understanding of the functions of social pretend play stimulate further thought and research.

Notes

1. Joseph Becker suggested that the Soviet notion of activity and dominant activity was relevant to this argument.

2. This study was supported by the Organization of American States, PRA Training Fellowship. The author gratefully thanks the American families who participated in this research. A special thanks is extended to the Mexican families of Bucerias, Nayarit.

3. The small number of embedded conflicts and the small number of children with insecure attachment histories who engaged in social pretend play preclude statistical analyses of these data.

References

Adler, L., and L. M. McCune. 1985. *Variations in mother-infant interaction: Relationships with symbolic development.* Unpublished manuscript, Douglas College, Rutgers University, New Brunswick, NJ.

Ainsworth, M., M. Blehar, E. Waters, and S. Wall. 1978. *Patterns of attachment.* Hillsdale, NJ: Erlbaum.

Arend, R. R., F. Gove, and L. A. Sroufe. 1979. Continuity of individual adaptation from infancy to kindergarten: A predictive study of ego-resiliency and curiosity in preschoolers. *Child Development* 50: 950–959.

Asher, S. R., and J. M. Gottman, eds. 1981. *The development of children's friendships.* New York: Cambridge University Press.

Asher, S. R., L. C. Singleton, B. R. Tinsley, and S. Hymel. 1979. A reliable sociometric measure for preschool children. *Developmental Psychology* 15: 443–444.

Bascom, W. 1969. *The Yourba of southwest Nigeria.* New York: Reinhart.

Bateson, G. 1971. The message this is play. In R. Herron and B. Sutton-Smith (eds.), *Child's play.* New York: Wiley.

Beitel, A., and R. D. Parke. 1985. *Relationships between preschoolers, sociometric factors and emotional decoding ability.* Unpublished manuscript, University of Illinois, Champaign-Urbana.

Belsky, J. 1983. The origins of individual differences in mother-infant attachment. *Child Development* 54: 83–96.

Belsky, J., L. Garduque, and E. Hrncir. 1984. Assessing performance, competence, and executive capacity in infant play: Relations to home environment and security of attachment. *Developmental Psychology* 20: 406–417.

Belsky, J., and R. Most. 1984. From exploration to play: A cross-sectional study of infant free play behavior. *Developmental Psychology* 17: 630–639.

Berg, M., and E. A. Medrich. 1980. Children in four neighborhoods: The physical environment and its effect on play and play patterns. *Environment and Behavior* 12: 320–348.

Berndt, T., J. A. Hawkins, and S. G. Hoyle. 1986. Changes in friendship during a school year: Effects on children's and adolescent's impressions of friendship and sharing with friends. *Child Development* 57: 1284–1297.

Bhavnagri, N. 1987. *Parents as faciliators of preschool children's peer relationships.* Ph.D. diss., University of Illinois, Champaign-Urbana.

Bowlby, J. 1973. *Attachment and loss* Vol. 2, *Separation.* New York: Basic Books.

Brenner, J., and E. Mueller. 1982. Shared meaning in boy toddlers' peer relations. *Child Development* 53: 380–391.

Bretherton, I. 1984. Representing the social world in symbolic play: Reality and fantasy. In I. Bretherton (ed.), *Symbolic play* (p. 144). New York: Academic Press.

Bretherton, I. 1985. Attachment theory: Retrospective and prospect. In I. Bretherton and E. Waters (eds.), *Growing points in attachment theory* (Vol. 50, No. 209, p. 33). Monographs of the Society for Research in Child Development.

Bretherton, I. 1987. *Pretense: The form and function of make-believe play.* Paper presented at the biennial meeting of the Society for Research in Child Development, April, in Baltimore, Maryland.

Bretherton, I., E. Bates, L. Benigini, L. Camaioni, and V. Volterra. 1979. Relationships between cognition, communication, and quality of attachment. In E. Bates, L. Benigini, I. Bretherton, L. Camaioni, and V. Volterra (eds.), *The emergence of symbols* (pp. 223–270). New York: Academic Press.

Bretherton, I., B. O'Connell, C. Shore, and E. Bates. 1984. The effect of contextual variation on symbolic play: Development from 20 to 28 months. In I. Bretherton (ed.), *Symbolic play* (pp. 271–298). New York: Academic Press.

Bretherton, I., D. Ridgeway, and J. Cassidy. In press. The role of internal working models in the attachment relationships: Can it be studied in three-year-olds. In M. Greenberg, D. Cicchetti, and E. M. Cummings (eds.), *Attachment during the preschool years: Theory, research and intervention.* Chicago: The University of Chicago Press.

Bridges, L. J., J. P. Connell, and J. Belsky. 1988. Similarities and differences in infant-mother and infant-father interaction in the strange situation: A component process analysis. *Developmental Psychology* 24: 92–100.

Brownell, C. 1986. Convergent developments: Cognitive-developmental correlates of growth in infant/toddler peer skills. *Child Development* 57: 275–286.

Bruner, J. 1978. Learning to do things with words. In J. Bruner and A. Garton (eds.), *Human growth and development.* Oxford: Oxford University Press.

Bryant, B. 1989. The need for support in relation to the need for autonomy. In D. Belle (ed.), *Social support across the life span* (pp. 332–351). Norwood, NJ: Ablex.

Centner, T. 1962. *L'enfant African et ses jeuz*. Elizabethville, CEPSI.

Cochran, M. M., and J. A. Brassard. 1979. Child development and personal social networks. *Child Development* 50: 601–616.

Coie, J. D., and K. A. Dodge. 1983. Continuities and changes in children's social status: A five year longitudinal study. *Merrill Palmer Quarterly* 29: 261–282.

Connolly, J., and A. Doyle. 1984. Relation of social fantasy play to social competence in preschoolers. *Developmental Psychology* 20: 797–806.

Connolly, J. A., A. Doyle, and E. Reznick. 1988. Social pretend play and social interaction in preschool. *Journal of Applied Developmental Psychology* 9: 301–313.

Conte, J. D., and K. A. Dodge. 1983. The impact of sexual abuse on children: Empirical findings. In L. E. A. Walker (ed.), *Handbook on sexual abuse of children* (pp. 102–134). New York: Wiley.

Cook-Gumperez, J., and W. Corsaro. 1977. Social-ecological constraints on children's communicative strategies. *Sociology* 11: 411–434.

Corsaro, W. A. 1981. Friendship in the nursery school. In S. R. Asher and J. Gottman (eds.), *The development of children's friendships* (pp. 207–241). New York: Cambridge University Press.

Corsaro, W. A. 1983. Script recognition, articulation, and expansion in children's role play. *Discourse Processes* 6: 1–19.

Corsaro, W. A. 1985. *Friendship and peer culture in the early years*. Norwood, NJ: Ablex.

Corsaro, W. A. 1986. Discourse processes within peer culture: From a constructivist to an interpretative approach to childhood socialization. In P. Adler (ed.), *Sociological studies of child development*. New York: JAI Press.

Corsaro, W., and G. Tomlinson. 1979. Spontaneous play and social learning. In A. Salter (ed.), *Play: Anthropological perspectives*. New York: Leisure Press.

DeLoache, J., and B. Plaetzer. 1985. *Tea for two: Joint mother-child symbolic play*. Paper presented at the biennial meeting of the Society for Research in Child Development.

Dodge, K. A. 1985. Facets of social interaction and the assessment of social competence in children. In B. H. Schneider, K. H. Rubin, and J. E. Ledingham (eds.), *Children's Peer Relations: Issues in Assessment and Intervention* (pp. 3–22). New York: Springer-Verlag.

Doyle, A., and J. Connolly. 1989. Negotiation and enactment in social pretend play: Relations to social acceptance and social cognition. *Early Childhood Research Quarterly* 4: 289–302.

Doyle, A. B., J. Connolly, and L. P. Rivest. 1979. The effect of playmate familiarity on the social interactions of young children. *Child Development* 51: 217–223.

Dunn, J., and N. Dale. 1984. I a daddy: Two-year-olds collaboration in joint pretend with a sibling and with a mother. In I. Bretherton (ed.), *Symbolic play* (pp. 131–158). New York: Academic Press.

Dunn, J., and P. Wooding. 1979. Play in the home and its implications for learning. In B. Tizzard and D. Harvey (eds.), *The biology of play* (pp. 45–58). London: Spastics International Medical Publications/Heinemann Medical Books.

Easterbrook, A., and M. Lamb. 1979. The relationship between quality of infant-mother attachment and infant competence in initial encounters with peers. *Child Development* 50: 380–387.

Eckerman, C. O., and J. L. Whatley. 1977. Toys and social interaction between infant peers. *Child Development* 48: 1645–1656.

Eckerman, C., and S. Didow. 1989. Toddler's social coordination: Changing responses to another's invitation to play. *Developmental Psychology* 25: 794–804.

Eckerman, C. O., C. C. Davis, and S. M. Didow. 1989. Toddler's emerging ways of achieving social coordination with a peer. *Child Development* 60: 440–453.

Elias, M. J., and M. Ubriaco. 1986. Linking parental beliefs to children's social competence: Toward a cognitive-behavioral assessment model. In R. D. Ashmore and D. M. Brodzinsky (eds.), *Thinking about the family.* New Jersey: Lawrence Erlbaum.

Erikson, E. H. 1950. *Childhood and society.* New York: Norton.

Erikson, E. H. 1964. *Insight and responsibility: Lectures on the ethical implications of psychoanalytic insight.* New York: Norton.

Farver, J. 1989. Communicating shared meaning in spontaneous fantasy play (under review).

Farver, J. 1989. *The development of symbolic play in Mexican and American Children.* Unpublished dissertation, University of California, Los Angeles.

Fein, G. 1979. Play and the acquisition of symbols. In L. Katz (ed.), *Current topics in early childhood education VII.* Norwood, NJ: Ablex.

Fein, G. 1981. Pretend play in childhood. *Child Development* 52: 1095–1118.

Fein, G. 1985. The affective psychology of play. In C. C. Brown and A. Gottfried (eds.), *Play interactions: The role of play toys, and parental involvement in children's development* (pp. 1928). Skillman, NJ: Johnson and Johnson.

Fein, G. 1985. A transformational analysis of pretending. *Developmental Psychology* 11: 291–296.

Fein, G. G. 1987. *Affective themes in the pretense of master players.* Paper presented at the biennial meeting of the Society for Research in Child Development.

Fein, G., E. Moorin, and J. Enslein. 1982. Pretense and peer behavior: An intersectoral analysis. *Human Development* 25: 392–406.

Fein, G., and S. Schwartz. 1986. The social coordination of pretense in preschool children. In G. Fein (ed.), *The young child at play.* Washington, D.C.: NAEYC.

Fenson, L. 1984. Developmental trends for action and speech in pretend play. In I. Bretherton (ed.), *Symbolic play* (pp. 249–270). New York: Academic.

Fenson, L., J. Kagan, R. B. Kearsley, and P. R. Zelazo. 1976. The developmental progression of manipulative play in the first two years. *Child Development* 47: 232–235.

Fenson, L., and D. Ramsay, 1980. Decentralization and the integration of play in the second of life. *Child Development* 51: 171–178.

Field, T., D. DeSatano, and P. Koewler, 1982. Fantasy play of toddlers and preschoolers. *Developmental Psychology* 18: 503–508.

Fiese, B. H. 1990. Playful relationships: A contextual analysis of mother-toddler interaction and symbolic play. *Child Development* 61: 1648–1656.

Fiese, B. H. 1989. *Creating the zone of proximal development: Lessons from the study of symbolic play.* Paper presented at the Biennial Meeting at the Society for Research in Child Development, April.

Foot, H. C., A. Chapman, and J. Smith. 1980. Patterns of interaction in children's friendships. In H. C. Foot, A. Chapman and J. Smith (eds.), *Friendship and social relations in young children* (pp. 267–293). New York: Wiley.

Forys, S. K. S., and L. McCune-Nicolich. 1984. Shared pretend: Sociodramatic play at three years of age. In I. Bretherton, (ed.), *Symbolic play: The development of social understanding* (pp. 159–194). New York: Academic Press.

Furman, W., and D. Buhrmester. 1985. Children's perceptions of the personal relationships in their social networks. *Developmental Psychology* 21: 1016–1024.

Galluzzo, D. C., C. C. Matheson, J. Moore, and C. Howes. 1988. Social orientation to adults and peers in infant child care. *Early Childhood Research Quarterly* 3(4), 417–426.

Garvey, C. 1974. Some properties of social play. *Merrill-Palmer Quarterly* 20: 163–180.

Garvey, C. 1977. *Play*. Cambridge: Harvard University Press.

Garvey, C. 1982. Communications and the development of social role play. In D. Forbes and M. Greenberg (eds.), *New directions in child development: Children's planning strategies* (pp. 81–102). San Francisco: Jossey-Bass.

Garvey, C. 1984. *Children's talk*. Oxford: Fontana.

Garvey, C., and R. Berndt. 1977. *Organization of pretend play*. Paper presented at the annual meeting of the American Psychological Association.

Gearhart, M. 1983. *Social plans and social episodes: The development of collaboration in role playing*. Unpublished dissertation, City University of New York.

Genishi, C. 1983. *Role initiation in the discourse of Mexican-American children's play*. Paper presented at the annual meeting of the American educational Research Association, Montreal, Canada, in April.

George, C., and M. Main. 1979. Social interactions of young abused children: Approach, avoidance, and aggression. *Child Development* 50: 306–318.

Goncu, A. 1987. *The dynamics of collaboration in the play of preschool children*. Paper presented at the biennial meeting of the Society for Research in Child Development.

Goncu, A., and F. Kessel. 1984. Children's play a contextual-functional perspective. In F. Kessel (ed.), *Analyzing children's play dialogues* (p. 522). New Directions in Child Development Research, San Francisco: Jossey-Bass.

Gottman, J. 1983. How children become friends. *Monograph of the Society for Research in Child Development* 48(201).

Gottman, J. 1986. The world of coordinated play: Same and cross sex friendships in young children. In J. Gottman and J. Parker (eds), *Conversations of friends: Speculations on affective development* (pp. 139–191). Cambridge: Cambridge University Press.

Gottman, J., and G. Mettetal. 1986. Speculations about social and affective development: Friendship and acquaintanceship through adolescence. In J. Gottman and J. Parker (eds.), *Conversations of friends: Speculations on affective development* (pp. 192–240). Cambridge: Cambridge University Press.

Gottman, J., and J. Parkhurst. 1980. A developmental theory of friendship and acquaintanceship processes. In A. Collins (ed.), *Development of cogni-*

tion affect and social relations. Minnesota Symposium of Child Psychology. Norwood, NJ: Erlbaum.

Green, J. A., G. E. Gustafson, and M. J. West. 1980. Effects of infant development on mother-infant interactions. *Child Development* 51: 199–207.

Griffin, H. 1984. The coordination of meaning in the creation of shared make believe reality. In I. Bretherton (ed.), *Symbolic play* (pp. 73–100). New York: Academic Press.

Gurian, A., and R. Formanek. 1983. *The socially competent child: A parent's guide to social development from infancy to early adolescence*. Boston: Houghton Mifflin Company.

Gustafson, G. E., J. A. Green, and M. J. West. 1979. The infant's changing role in mother-infant games: The growth of social skills. *Infant Behavior and Development* 2: 301–308.

Halverson, C. F., Jr., and M. F. Waldrop. 1970. Maternal behavior toward own and other preschool children: The problem of "ownness." *Child Development* 41: 839–845.

Harms, T., and R. Clifford. 1980. *Early childhood environment rating scale*. New York: Teachers College Press, Columbia University.

Hartup, W. W. 1979. The social worlds of childhood. *American Psychologist* 34: 944–950.

Hartup, W. W. 1983a. Peer relations. In P. H. Mussen (Series ed.), E. M. Hetherington (Vol. ed.), *Handbook of child psychology, Vol. 4, socialization, personality, and social development* (pp. 103–196). New York: Wiley.

Hartup, W. W. 1983b. The peer system. In E. M. Hetherington and P. Mussen (eds.), *Handbook of child psychology: Socialization, personality, and social development* (Vol. 4, pp. 103–196). New York: Wiley.

Hartup, W. W. 1989. Behavioral manifestations of children's friendships. In T. J. Berndt and G. W. Ladd (eds.), *Peer relationships in child development* (pp. 46–67). New York: Wiley.

Hartup, W. W., B. Laursen, M.I. Stewart, and A. Eastenson. 1988. Conflict and the friendship relations of young children. *Child Development* 59: 1590–1600.

Hay, D. 1985. Learning to form relationships in infancy: Parallel attainment with parents and peers. *Developmental Review* 5: 122–161.

Hill, P., and L. McCune. 1981. Pretend play and patterns of cognitions in Down Syndrome children. *Child Development* 52: 611617.

Hinde, R. A., G. Titmus, J. Easton, and A. Tamplin. 1985. Incidence of friendship and behavior towards strong associates vs. nonassociates in preschools. *Child Development* 55: 234–245.

Hodapp, R., E. Goldfield, and C. Boyatzis. 1984. The use and effectiveness of maternal scaffolding in mother-infant games. *Child Development* 55: 772–781.

Hodapp, R. M., and E. C. Goldfield. 1985. Self and other-regulation during the infancy period. *Developmental Review* 5: 274–288.

Hoofman-Plotkin, D., and C. Twentyman. 1984. A multimodal assessment of behavior and cognitive deficits in abused and neglected preschoolers. *Child Development* 55: 794–802.

Howes, C. 1983. Patterns of friendship. *Child Development* 54: 1041–1053.

Howes, C. 1985. Sharing fantasy: Social pretend in toddlers. *Child Development* 56: 1253–1258.

Howes, C. 1987. Social competence with peers in young children: Developmental sequences. *Developmental Review* 7: 252–272.

Howes, C. 1988. Peer interaction in young children. *Monograph of the Society for Research in Child Development: #217 (Vol. 53, No. 1)*.

Howes, C., and R. Eldredge. 1985. Responses of abused, neglected, and non-maltreated children to the behaviors of their peers. *Journal of Applied Developmental Psychology* 6: 261–270.

Howes, C., and J. Farver. 1987. Social pretend play in two-year-olds: Effects of age of partners. *Early Childhood Research Quarterly* 2: 305–315.

Howes, C., and F. Wu. 1990. Peer interactions and friendships in an ethnically diverse school setting. *Child Development* 61: 537–541.

Howes, C., and O. Unger. 1989. Play with peers in child care settings. In M. Bloch and A. Pellegrini (eds.), *The ecological context of children's play* (pp. 104–119). Norwalk, NJ: Ablex.

Howes, C., O. Unger, and L. Seidner. 1989. Social pretend play in toddlers: Social pretend play forms and parallels with solitary pretense. *Child Development* 60: 132–158.

Howes, C., C. Rodning, D. Galluzzo, and L. Meyers. 1988. Attachment and child care: Relationships with mother and caregiver. *Early Childhood Research Quarterly* 3: 403–416.

Hymel, S. 1983. Preschool children's peer relations: Issues in sociometric assessment. *Merrill Palmer Quarterly* 29: 237–260.

Iwanaga, M. 1973. Development of interpersonal play structures in three four- and five-year-old children. *Journal of Research and Development in education: 671–682*.

Jackowitz, E., and M. Watson. 1980. Development of object transformations in early pretend play. *Developmental Psychology* 16: 543–549.

Johnson, J. E., J. F. Christie, T. D. Yawkey. 1987. *Play and early childhood development.* Glenview, IL. Scott, Foresman and Company.

Kavanaugh, R. D., S. Whittington, and M. J. Cerbone. 1983. Mothers' use of fantasy in speech to young children. *Journal of Child Language* 10: 45–55.

Keenan, E. 1974. Conversational competence in children. *Journal of Child Language* 1: 163–183.

Kopp, C. 1982. The antecedents of self regulation. *Developmental Psychology* 18: 199–214.

Ladd, G., and B. Golter. 1988. Parents' management of preschooler's peer relations: Is it related to children's social competence? *Developmental Psychology* 24: 109–117.

Ladd, G. W., C. H. Hart, E. M. Wadsworth, and B. S. Golter. 1988. Preschoolers' peer networks in nonschool settings: Relationships to family characteristics and school adjustment. In S. Salzinger, J., Antrobus, and M. Hammer (eds.), *Social networks of children, adolescents and college students.* Hillsdale, NJ: Erlbaum.

LaFreniere, P., and L. A. Sroufe. 1985. Profiles of peer competence in preschool: Interrelations between measures, influence of social ecology, and relation to attachment history. *Developmental Psychology* 21: 265–275.

Lamb, M., C. P. Hwang, A. Frodi, and M. Frodi. 1982. Security of mother- and father-infant attachment and its relation to sociability with strangers in traditional and nontraditional Swedish families. *Infant Behavior and Development* 5: 355–367.

Lamb, M. E. 1976. Twelve-month-olds and their parents: Interaction in a laboratory playroom. *Developmental Psychology* 12: 237–244.

Lamb, M. E., R. A. Thompson, W. Gardner, and .E. L. Charnov. 1985. *Infant-mother attachment: The origins and developmental significance of individual differences in strange situation behavior.* Hillsdale, NJ: Erlbaum.

Lancy, D. F. 1977. The play behavior of Kpelle children during rapid cultural change. In D. Lancy and B. Tinball (eds.), *The study of play.* New York: Leisure Press.

Largo, R., and J. Howard. 1979a. Developmental progression in play behaviors between 9 and 30 months. *Developmental Medicine and Child Neurology* 21: 299–310.

Largo, R. H., and S. A. Howard. 1979b. Developmental progressions in play behavior of children between nine and thirty months. I: Spontaneous play and language development. *Developmental Medicine and Neurology* 21: 492–504.

Laursen, B., and W. W. Hartup. 1989. The dynamics of preschool children's conflicts. *Merrill Palmer Quarterly* 35: 281–297.

Laursen, B., and W. W. Hartup. 1989. The dynamics of preschool children's conflicts. *Merrill Palmer Quarterly* 35: 281–297.

Lederberg, A. R., S. Rosenblatt, D. L. Vandell, and S. Chapin. 1987. Temporary and long term friendships in hearing and deaf preschoolers. *Merrill Palmer Quarterly* 33: 515–534.

Levin, H., and R. R. Sears. 1956. Identification with parents as a determinant of doll play aggression. *Child Development* 27: 135–153.

Levin, H., and E. Wardwell. 1962. The research uses of doll play. *Psychological Bulletin* 59: 27–56.

Lewis, M., C. Feiring, C. McGuffog, and J. Jaskir. 1984. Predicting psychopathology in six year olds from early social relations. *Child Development* 55: 123–136.

Lezine, I. 1973. The transition from sensorimotor to earliest symbolic function in development. *Early Development, Research Publication ARNMD* 51: 22–232.

Lisina, M. I. 1985. *Child-adults-peers*. Moscow: Progress Publishers.

Lowe, M. 1975. Trends in the development of representational play in infants from one to three years: An observational study. *Journal of Child Psychology and Psychiatry* 16: 33–47.

MacDonald, K., and R. D. Parke. 1985. Bridging the gap: Parent-child play interactions and peer interactive competence. *Child Development* 55: 932–940.

Macoby, E. E., and J. A. Martin. 1983. Socialization in the context of the family: Parent-child interaction. In P. H. Mussen (ed.) *Handbook of child psychology*. New York: John Wiley and Sons.

Main, M., and D. R. Weston. 1981. The quality of the toddler's relationship to the mother and to the father: Related to conflict behavior and the readiness to establish new relationships. *Child Development* 52: 932–940.

Main, M., N. Kaplan, and J. Cassidy. 1985. Security in infancy, childhood, and adulthood: A move to the level of representation. In I. Bretherton and E. Waters (eds.), Growing Points in Attachment. *Monographs of the Society for Research in Child Development* 50: (Serial No. 209).

Master, J. C., and W. C. Furman. 1981. Popularity, individual friendship selection and specific peer interaction among children. *Developmental Psychology* 17: 344–350.

Matas, L., R. Arend, and L. A. Sroufe. 1978. Continuity of adaptation in the second year: The relationship between quality of attachment and later competence. *Child Development* 49: 547–556.

Mathews, W. S. 1977. Modes of transformation in the initiation of fantasy play. *Developmental Psychology* 13: 212–216.

McCune-Nicolich, L. 1981. Towards symbolic functioning: Structure of early pretend games and potential parallels with language. *Child Development* 52: 785–797.

McGillicuddy-De Lisi, A. V. 1985. The relationship between parental beliefs and children's cognitive level. In I. E. Sigel (ed.) *Parental belief Systems* (pp. 144–159). Hillsdale, NJ: Erlbaum.

McLoyd, V. 1980. Verbally expressed modes of transformation in the fantasy play of black preschool children. *Child Development* 51: 1133–1139.

McLoyd, V., D. Warren, and E. Thomas. 1984. Anticipatory and fantastic role enactment in preschool triads. *Developmental Psychology* 20: 807–814.

Miller, P., and C. Garvey. 1984. Mother-baby role play: Its origins in social support. In I. Bretherton (ed.), *Symbolic play: The development of social understanding* (pp. 101–130). New York: Academic Press.

Miller, S. A. 1988. Parents' beliefs about children's cognitive development. *Child Development* 59: 259–286.

Mueller, E. 1972. The maintenance of verbal exchanges between young children. *Child Development* 43: 930–938.

Mueller, E., M. Bleier, J. Krakow, K. Hegedus, and P. Cournoyer. 1977. The development of peer verbal interaction among two-year-old boys. *Child Development* 48: 248–287.

Mueller, E., and J. Brenner. 1977. The origins of social skills and interaction among play-group toddlers. *Child Development* 48: 854–861.

Nadel, J., and A. M. Fontaine. 1989. Communicating by imitation: A developmental and comparative approach to transitory social competence. In B. Schneider et al. (eds.), *The development of social competence* (pp. 131–144). Dordrecht: Kleuwer.

Nelson, K., and S. Seidman. 1984. Playing with scripts. In I. Bretherton (ed.), *Symbolic play* (pp. 45–72). New York: Academic Press.

Newcomb, A. F., and W. M. Bukowski. 1983. Social impact and social preference as determinants of children's peer group status. *Developmental Psychology* 19: 856–867.

Nicolich, L. 1977. Beyond sensorimotor intelligence: Assessment of symbolic maturity through analysis of pretend play. *Merrill-Palmer Quarterly* 23: 89–101.

O'Connell, B., and I. Bretherton. 1984. Toddler's play alone and with mother: The role of maternal guidance. In I. Bretherton (ed.), *Symbolic play* (pp. 337–366). Orlando, FL: Academic Press.

O'Connell, B. G., and A. B. Gerard. 1985. Scripts and scraps: The development of sequential understanding. *Child Development* 56: 671–681.

Oppenheim, D. 1987. *Preschooler's representations of attachment issues in a doll play interview.* Paper presented at the Biennial Meeting of the Society for Research in Child Development, Baltimore, MD.

Oppenheim, D. 1989. *Assessing preschoolers' security of attachment using a doll interview.* Paper presented at the Biennial Meeting of the Society for Research in Child Development, Kansas City, MO.

Oppenheim, D., A. Sagi, and M. Lamb. 1988. Infant-adult attachments on the kibbutz and their relation to socioemotional development four years later. *Developmental Psychology* 24: 427–433.

Paley, V. G. 1984. *Boys and girls: Super heros in the doll corner.* Chicago: The University of Chicago Press.

Paley, V. G. 1986. *Mollie is three: Growing up in school.* Chicago: The University of Chicago Press.

Paley, V. G. 1988. *Bad guys don't have birthdays: Fantasy play at four.* Chicago: The University of Chicago Press.

Park, K. A., and E. Waters. 1989. Security of attachment and preschool friendships. *Child Development* 60: 1076–1081.

Parke, R. D. 1978. Children's home environments: Social and cognitive effects. In I. Altman and J. R. Wohlwill (eds.), *Children and the environment: New York: Plenum.*

Parke, R. D., and N. P. Bhavnagri. 1988. Parents as managers of children's peer relationships. In D. Belle (ed.), *Children's social networks and social supports.* New York: Wiley.

Parke, R. D., K. B. MacDonald, A. Beitel, and N. Bhavnagri. In press. The role of the family in the development of peer relationships. In R. DeV. Peters and R. J. McMahan (eds.), *Marriage and families: Behavioral treatments and processes.* New York: Brunner-Mazel.

Parker, J. G., and J. M. Gottman. 1989. Social and emotional development in a relational context: Friendship interaction from early childhood to adolescence. In T. J. Berndt and G. W. Ladd (eds.), *Peer relationships in child development* (pp. 95–131). New York: Wiley.

Pellegrini, A. D. 1985. The narrative organization of children's fantasy play: The effects of age and play context. *educational Psychology* 5: 17–25.

Perry, J. C. 1979. Popular, amiable, isolated, rejected: A reconceptualization of sociometric status in preschool children. *Child Development* 50: 1231–1234.

Raum, O. 1940. *Chaga childhood.* London: Oxford University Press

Reidy, T. J. 1977. The aggressive characteristics of abused and neglected children. *Journal of Clinical Psychology* 33: 1140–1145.

Roopnarine, J., and T. Field. 1984. Play interactions of friends and acquaintances in nursery school. In T. Field, J. Roopnarine, and M. Segal (eds.), *Friendship in normal and handicapped children* (pp. 89–98). Norwalk, NJ: Ablex.

Rose-Krasnor, L. 1983. An observational study of social problem solving in young children. In. K. H. Rubin and H. S. Ross (eds.), *Peer relationships and social skills in childhood* (pp. 113–132). New York: Springer Verlag.

Rosenberg, D. M. 1983. *The quality and content of preschool fantasy play: Correlates in concurrent social-personality functioning and early mother-child attachment relationship.* Unpublished doctoral dissertation, University of Minnesota.

Ross, H. 1982. Establishment of social games among toddlers. *Developmental Psychology* 18: 509–518.

Ross, H., and D. Kay. 1980. The origins of social games. *New Directions for Child Development* 9: 17–31.

Ross, H. S., and S. P. Lollis. In press. A social relations analysis of toddler peer relationships, *Child Development.*

Ross, H. S., J. A. Cheyne, and S. P. Lollis, 1988. Defining and studying reciprocity in young children. In S. Duck (ed.), *Handbook of social relationships: (pp. 143–160). Chichester: Wiley.*

Rubin, K. H. 1980. Fantasy play: Its role in the development of social skills and social cognition. In K. H. Rubin (ed.), *Children's play.* San Francisco: Jossey-Bass.

Rubin, K. H., G. Fein, and B. Vandenberg. 1983. Play. In E. M. Hetherington (ed.), *Socialization, personality, and social development: Handbook of child psychology* (Vol. IV). New York: Wiley.

Rubin, K. H., and L. Krasnor. 1986. Social-cognitive and social behavioral perspectives on problem solving. In M. Permutter (ed.), *Cognitive perspectives on children's social and behavioral development.* Minnesota Symposia on Child Psychology, Vol. 18. Hillsdale, NJ: Erlbaum.

Rubin, Z. 1980. *Children's friendships.* Cambridge: Harvard University Press

Rubin, Z., and J. Sloman. 1984. How parents influence their children's friendships. In M. Lewis (ed.), *Beyond the dyad.* New York: Plenum Press.

Sachs, J., J. Goldman, and C. Chaille. 1984. Planning in pretend play: Using language to coordinate narrative development. In A. Pellegrini and T. Yawkey (eds.), *The development of oral and written language in social context.* Norwalk, NJ: Ablex.

Sachs, J. 1980. The role of adult-child play in language development. *New Directions for Child Development* 9: 33–47.

Sachs, J., J. Goldman, and C. Chaille. 1985. Narratives in preschooler's sociodramatic play: The role of knowledge in communicative competence. In L. Galda and A. D. Pelegrini (eds.), *Play, language, and story: The development of children's literate behavior.* Norwalk, NJ: Ablex.

Salzinger, S., J. Antrobus and M. Hammer. (eds.) 1988. *Social networks of children, adolescents and college students.* Hillsdale, NJ: Erlbaum.

Salzinger, S., and J. Hampson. 1988. Social networks of mother and child: An examination of their function in developing speech. In S. Salzinger, J. Antrobus, and M. Hammer (eds.), *Social networks of children, adolescents and college Students.* Hillsdale, NJ: Lawrence Erlbaum.

Saxe, G. B., M. Gearhart, and S. R. Guberman. 1984. The social organization of early number development. *New Directions for Child Development* 23: 19–30.

Saxe, G., S. Guberman, and M. Gearhart. 1987. Social processes in early number development. Monographs for the Society of Research in *Child Development* 216.

Saunders, K., and L. Harper. 1976. Free play fantasy behavior in preschool children: Relations among gender, age, season, and location. *Child Development* 47: 1182–1185.

Schaffer, H. R., and C. K. Crook, 1979. Maternal control techniques in a directed play situation. *Child Development* 50: 989–998.

Schaffer, H. R. 1984. *The child's entry into a social world.* New York: Academic.

Schwartzman, H. 1976. The anthropology of children's play. *Annual Review of Anthropology* 5: 219–328.

Schwartzman, H. 1978. *Transformations: The anthropology of children's play.* New York: Plenum Press.

Segal, M., J. Peck, N. Vega-Lahr, and T. Field. 1987. A medieval kingdom: Leader-follower styles of preschool play. *Journal of Applied Developmental Psychology* 8: 79–95.

Seidman, S. 1983. *Eventful play: preschoolers' scripts for pretense.* Paper presented at SRCD, Detroit, Michigan.

Shantz, C. U. 1987. Conflicts between children. *Child Development* 58: 283–305.

Shaw, V. L., and J. H. Meier. 1983. *The effect of type of abuse and neglect on children's psychosocial development.* Unpublished manuscript, Children's Village, USA.

Sigel, I. E. 1986. Reflections on the belief-behavior connection: Lessons learned from a research program on parental belief systems and teaching strategies. In R. D. Ashmore and D. M. Brodzinsky (eds.), *Thinking about the family: Views of parents and children* (pp. 35–65). Hillsdale, NJ: Erlbaum.

Singer, J. L. 1973. *The child's world of make-believe*. New York: Academic Press.

Slade, A. 1987a. Quality of attachment and early symbolic play. *Developmental Psychology* 23: 78–85.

Slade, A. 1987b. A longitudinal study of maternal involvement and symbolic play during the toddler period. *Child Development* 58: 367–375.

Smilansky, S. 1968. *The effects of sociodramatic play on disadvantaged preschool children*. New York, New York: Wiley.

Sroufe, L. A. 1983. Infant-caregiver attachment and patterns of adaptation in preschool: The roots of maladaptation and competence. In M. Perlmutter (ed.), *Minnesota Symposium in Child Psychology* (Vol. 16). Hillsdale, NJ: Erlbaum.

Storey, K. S. 1976. Field study: Children's play in Bali. In D. F. Lancy and A. Tinball (eds.), *The anthropological study of play problems and prospects* (pp. 66–72). New York: Leisure Press.

Tessier, O., and M. Boivin. 1985. *The coherence of sociometric nominations and the preschooler's understanding of friendship*. Paper presented at the biennial meeting of the Society for Research in Child Development, Toronto, April.

Unger, O., and C. Howes. 1988. Mother-child interaction and symbolic play between toddlers and their adolescent or mentally retarded mothers. *The Occupational Therapy Journal of Research* 8: 237–249.

Vandell, D. L., and E. Mueller. 1980. Peer play and friendships during the first two years. In H. C. Foot, A. Chapman and J. Smith (eds.), *Friendship and social relations in young children* (pp. 294–317). New York: Wiley.

Vygotsky, L. S. 1962. *Thought and language*. Cambridge: MIT Press.

Vygotsky, L. S. 1978a. Interaction between learning and development. In L. S. Vygotsky (ed.), *Mind in society*. Cambridge: MIT Press.

Vygotsky, L. S. 1978b. *Mind and society*. Cambridge: Harvard University Press.

Waters, E., and K. E. Deanne. 1985. Defining and assessing individual differences in attachment relationships. In I. Bretherton and E. Waters (eds.), Growing Points in Attachment Theory and Research. Monographs of the Society for Research in *Child Development* 50: 41–65.

Waters, E., J. Wippman, and L. A. Sroufe. 1979. Attachment, positive affect, and competence in the peer group: Two studies in construct validation. *Child Development* 50: 821–829.

Watson, M., and K. Fischer. 1980. Developmental of social roles in elicited and spontaneous behavior during the preschool years. *Developmental Psychology* 16: 483–494.

Watson, M., and K. Fischer. 1977. A developmental sequence of agent use in late infancy. *Child Development* 48: 828–836.

Wertsch, J. W. 1979. From social interaction to higher psychological processes: A clarification and application to Vygotsky's theory. *Human Development* 22: 1–22.

Wertsch, J. W., G. D. McName, J. B. McLane, and N. A. Budwig. 1980. The adult-child dyad as a problem-solving system. *Child Development* 51: 1215–1221.

Whiting, B., and .C. Edwards. 1988. *Children of different worlds: The formation of social behavior.* Cambridge: Harvard University Press.

Wolfe, D. 1982. Understanding others: A longitudinal case study of the concept of independent agency. In G. Foreman (ed.), *Action and thought: From sensorimotor to symbol use.* New York: Academic Press.

Wolhwil, W. 1973. *The study of behavioral development.* New York: Academic Press.

Wood, D., J. S. Bruner, and G. Ross. 1976. The role of tutoring in problem solving. *Journal of Child Psychology and Psychiatry* 17: 89–100.

Subject Index

Author Index